NATIONS OF THE WORLD

ITALY

Picot Cassidy

RAINTREE
STECK-VAUGHN
PUBLISHERS

A Harcourt Company

Austin   New York
www.steck-vaughn.com

Steck-Vaughn Company

First published 2002 by Raintree Steck-Vaughn Publishers,
an imprint of Steck-Vaughn Company.

Library of Congress Cataloging-in-Publication Data

Cassidy, Picot
    Italy / Picot Cassidy
       p. cm. -- (Nations of the world)
    Includes bibliographical references and index.
    ISBN 0-7398-1287-4
    1. Italy-- Juvenile literature. [1. Italy] I. Title. II. Nations of the world (Austin, Tex.)

DG417 .C37 2001
945

2001017052

Printed and bound in the United States
1 2 3 4 5 6 7 8 9 0   05 04 03 02 01

Brown Partworks Limited
Project Editor: Peter Jones
Designer: Joan Curtis, Seth Grimbly
Cartographer: William Le Bihan
Picture Researcher: Lizzie Clachan
Editorial Assistant: Anthony Shaw
Indexer: Kay Ollerenshaw

Raintree Steck-Vaughn
Publishing Director: Walter Kossmann
Art Director: Richard Johnson
Editors: Frank Tarsitano, Shirley Shalit

Front cover: Positano, Campania (background); Michelangelo's *Pietà* (right); Etruscan tomb painting (top left)
Title page: The Ponte Vecchio, Florence.

The acknowledgments on p. 128 form part of this copyright page.

Contents

Foreword

Since ancient times, people have gathered together in communities where they could share and trade resources and strive to build a safe and happy environment. Gradually, as populations grew and societies became more complex, communities expanded to become nations—groups of people who felt sufficiently bound by a common heritage to work together for a shared future.

Land has usually played an important role in defining a nation. People have a natural affection for the landscape in which they grew up. They are proud of its natural beauties—the mountains, rivers, and forests—and of the towns and cities that flourish there. People are proud, too, of their nation's history—the shared struggles and achievements that have shaped the way they live today.

Religion, culture, race, and lifestyle, too, have sometimes played a role in fostering a nation's identity. Often, though, a nation includes people of different races, beliefs, and customs. Many may have come from distant countries. Nations have rarely been fixed, unchanging things, either territorially or racially. Throughout history, borders have changed, often under the pressure of war, and people have migrated across the globe in search of a new life or because they are fleeing from oppression or disaster. The world's nations are still changing today: Some nations are breaking up and new nations are forming.

The Italian people have one of the richest cultures in the world. It is composed of many regional traditions that were previously part of independent states. The earliest of these were the Etruscan and Roman cultures that developed in central Italy, the latter the center of a vast civilization. Rome then achieved importance at the head of the Catholic church, and it was in the small city-states of the peninsula that the great flowering of art that was the Renaissance began. Although only formed into one nation in 1861, today Italy is a vibrant mix of its many parts, combining its historical dominance in the arts with contemporary excellence in design, fashion, agriculture, and fine food and wines.

Introduction

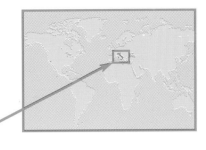

Many things come to mind when we think of Italy—tasty pizza and ice cream, elegant fashions and fast automobiles, romantic operas and fine art, to name just a few. Visitors to the country, though, remember Italy less for these individual things than for a general atmosphere—its beautiful old cities set amid lush countryside, its friendly, lively people, and, above all, its warm and sunny climate.

Italy has a central position in southern Europe. It covers an area of 116,293 square miles (301,268 sq. km), about the size of Nevada. Mainland Italy consists of a long, narrow peninsula, shaped roughly like a leg, which sticks right out into the Mediterranean Sea. There are also two large islands—Sicily and Sardinia—as well as other smaller islands. The largest island, Sicily, sits like a football on the "toe" of Italy. To the west of the mainland, at about "shin level," is the country's second-largest island, Sardinia. Italy's northern land borders are with France, Switzerland, Austria, and Slovenia. The country's southernmost point is the tiny island of Lampedusa, which lies closer to the North African country of Tunisia than to Italy.

Although the nation of Italy was only unified in 1861 (*see* pp. 66–68), the area now occupied by the country has had a profound effect on the history of Europe and of the whole world. Italy once stood at the center of the Roman

(*see* pp. 66–68)

Perhaps the greatest symbol of the Renaissance in architecture, Filippo Brunelleschi's dome of Florence cathedral dominates the city's skyline.

FACT FILE

- Italy only became one country in 1861. Foreign rule was ended in 1870.

- Between 1860 and 1973, 26 million Italians emigrated to other countries, especially to North and South America.

- Inside Italian territory are two independent republics—San Marino and the Vatican City.

- San Marino, which lies in the east of the Italian peninsula, is the oldest republic in the world, founded in the fourth century A.D. It covers only 24 square miles (62 sq. km) and has only 24,000 inhabitants.

The French emperor, Napoleon Bonaparte, made the tricolore the flag of the Italian areas he conquered in 1796, changing the blue of the French flag to green because it was his favorite color.

The lira was relatively unstable throughout the 1970s and early 1980s. It is hoped that the new euro will bring enduring economic stability.

empire, and 2,000 years ago the ancestors of the Italian people had one of the most sophisticated and productive civilizations of the ancient world. With the rise of Christianity the city of Rome became the center of the Catholic church, itself a major political as well as spiritual power. Later, in the 14th and 15th centuries Italy became the center of the artistic cultural rebirth of Europe known as the Renaissance, which developed in the small city-states of Italy, such as Florence and Pisa.

Today Italy is a major player in the European Union (EU). It is the sixth-largest economy in the world, and a leader in agriculture, automobile manufacture, fashion, and design. The country's historic artifacts make it a magnet for tourists. In addition Italy enjoys very varied terrain, from the snowy peaks of the Alps Mountains to the sun-drenched beaches of the south and the rich farming land of the central regions.

The flag of Italy has three vertical bands in green, white, and red. Italians sometimes call their flag the *tricolore* because it has three colors. It was modeled on the French flag, which is blue, white, and red. It became the official flag when Italy was united in 1861.

Italy's currency is called the lira, the plural is *lire*. One lira is not worth very much, so most prices are usually measured in thousands. For example, an ice-cream cone costs about 2,500 to 3,000 lire. The coins are in values of 50, 100, 200, 500, 1,000, and 2,000 lire. Bills are 1,000, 2,000, 5,000, 10,000, 50,000, and 100,000 lire. In 2002, the lira will be abolished. Countries of the European Union (EU) that are participating in the single currency such as Italy will use a new currency called the euro.

The official language of Italy is Italian. It is a Romance language, which means that it comes originally from Latin, the language spoken by the ancient Romans. Italian is also an official language in the Ticino, the part of southern Switzerland that borders on Italy. Before people spoke standard Italian—which is based on the dialect of Florence—people living in different areas of the Italian peninsula spoke their own dialects. Some of these dialects can be quite close to Italian, but they have some very different words. On the island of Sardinia, people speak Sard. At the beginning

The area around Bolzano is important as the center of the Ladin language. Descended from the Latin language, and once the mother tongue of the entire Tyrol, it now has only a few thousand speakers.

The National Anthem

The Italian national anthem, *"Fratelli d'Italia"* ("Brothers and Sisters of Italy"), was written before Italy became reunited as a country. It was officially adopted as the national anthem in 1948.

The words are by Goffredo Mameli (1827–1849), who died fighting for a united Italy. Two years before his death, he wrote the words. His friend Michele Novaro set the words to music. Mameli's song became very popular as a way of showing support for a united Italy, even when people could be arrested for singing it.

First verse
Brothers and sisters of Italy,
Italy has arisen,
With Scipio's helmet
Binding her head.
Where is Victory?

Let her bow down,
For God has made her
The slave of Rome.

Chorus
Let us gather in legions,
Ready to die!
Italy has called!

Second verse
We for centuries
Have been downtrodden and derided
Because we are not a people,
Because we are divided.
Let one flag, one hope
Bring us together;
The hour has struck
For us to join forces.
Let us gather in legions,
Ready to die!
Italy has called!

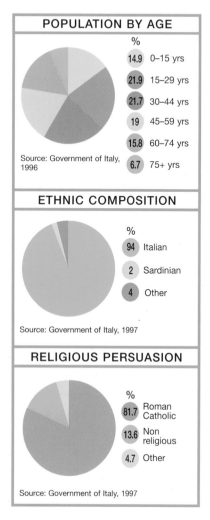

POPULATION BY AGE

%
14.9	0–15 yrs
21.9	15–29 yrs
21.7	30–44 yrs
19	45–59 yrs
15.8	60–74 yrs
6.7	75+ yrs

Source: Government of Italy, 1996

ETHNIC COMPOSITION

%
94	Italian
2	Sardinian
4	Other

Source: Government of Italy, 1997

RELIGIOUS PERSUASION

%
81.7	Roman Catholic
13.6	Non religious
4.7	Other

Source: Government of Italy, 1997

Italy has a remarkably uniform population, which is largely Catholic. Compared to other major European nations such as Britain and France, there has been relatively little recent immigration.

of the 20th century only 2 percent of Italians spoke exclusively Italian, the rest used local dialects for day-to-day speech. Today young people can often understand the local dialect, but they tend to speak it less than their grandparents or even their parents.

Other languages are also spoken in Italy. People living in border areas often speak the languages of the nearby countries. In the Aosta Valley, near France, around 100,000 people speak French. The northeastern region of Trentino-Alto Adige, near Austria, has around 200,000 German speakers. In the same region, Ladin and Friulian are spoken by people of the Southern Tyrol. Like Italian, these languages also derive from Latin. Farther east around Trieste, some people speak Slovenian. In the south of Italy, there are communities of Greeks and Albanians who settled in Italy in the 14th and 15th centuries, and still speak Greek and Albanian.

Religion

Most Italians are Roman Catholics, but there are also Protestant minorities in the far northeast of the country. Altogether Protestant groups number around 200,000 worshipers. The Jewish community has 35,000 members. There are also about 300,000 Muslims, mostly immigrants from Morocco, Tunisia, and Senegal, who tend to live in the south or the industrial cities of the north.

WHERE DOES ITALY'S POPULATION LIVE?

67%
Cities and towns

33%
Country

POPULATION DENSITY

Italy's population is largely clustered around its major cities, the industrial centers of Milan, Turin, and Genoa in the north and the two regional capitals of Rome and Naples in the center and south. During the industrial boom of the 1960s, large numbers of people from the agricultural south abandoned their poor farming lands in favor of the industrial suburbs of the north. Since the 1980s, the government has launched policies to encourage investment and population movement toward the south of the country.

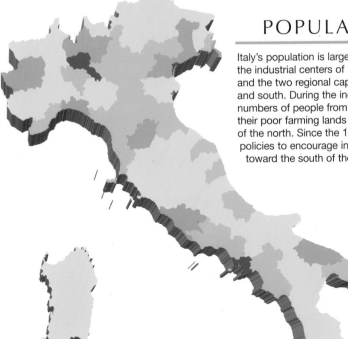

PERSONS

Per sq. mi		Per sq. km
13		5
65		25
130		50
520		200

Despite a rapid increase in the immediate postwar period, Italy's population has now leveled off and will soon go into decline.

National symbols

The national emblem of Italy was chosen in 1946, when Italy became a republic. It is a five-pointed white star superimposed on a cogwheel. Around the left side of the cogwheel are laurel leaves and to the right oak leaves. The star represents unity; the cogwheel, industry; and the leaves, republicanism. The national flower is the carnation. In addition to the national symbols many of the major towns also have historic emblems. Venice has the winged lion, Florence the lily, Rome the she-wolf suckling its cubs. These symbols reflect the history of these cities as independent states.

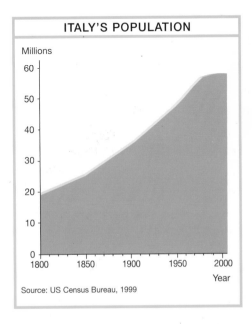

ITALY'S POPULATION

Millions

Year

Source: US Census Bureau, 1999

Land and Cities

"For wheresoe'er I turn my ravished eyes/Gay gilded scenes and shining prospects rise./Poetic fields encompass me around./And still I seem to walk on classic ground."

From *A Letter from Italy* by 17th-century English writer Joseph Addison

The nation of Italy is surrounded on three sides by the Mediterranean Sea. The country is largely mountainous. Low-lying areas comprise just 22 percent of the country. Nevertheless, there are a great variety of landscapes, including snow-capped peaks in the north, lush green hills in the center, and rocky coastal areas, especially in the south.

From north to south, the country stretches 745 miles (1,200 km). From side to side, however, it varies between only 87 miles (54 km) and 105 miles (170 km) wide. The land borders to the north are 1,198 miles (1,932 km) long. This is short in comparison to the coastline, which stretches for 4,723 miles (7,600 km). This figure includes the coastlines of the 3,766 islands that lie around Italy's mainland peninsula.

Italy lies in an earthquake zone, an area where the plates that make up Earth's crust sometimes push against each other. Beneath the plates is magma, a molten rock that can rise up to the surface as an eruption through a volcano. Central and southern Italy have more earthquakes and volcanoes than the north.

To a large extent the geographical differences between the northern Alpine region of Italy and the warmer southern region reflect differences between the Germanic culture of northern Europe and the more mixed Mediterranean culture of the south.

The composition of the Italian landscape, such as this area in Tuscany, has been an inspiration to artists for hundreds of years.

FACT FILE

- Italy is 78 percent hills or mountains, with many ranges over 2,300 feet (702m).

- The highest mountain in Italy is in the Monte Rosa massif (a large mountainous mass), on the Italian–Swiss border. Its tallest summit, the Dufourspitze, is 15,203 feet (4,634 m) high.

- Four seas wash the Italian coastline, all of which are part of the Mediterranean. The Ligurian Sea is off the west coast near Genoa, and the Adriatic Sea lies off the east coast. Between the mainland and the island of Sardinia is the Tyrrhenian Sea. The Ionian Sea lies east of Sicily.

ITALY'S TERRAIN

● **Plains**
Less than 25 percent of Italy is made up of plains and more than half of these lie in the Po Valley, the country's main agricultural region. In addition there are smaller lands down the Tuscan coast and around the cities of Naples and Rome on the west coast, largely areas of reclaimed swampland. In the southern region of Puglia are ancient plains leveled by the sea.

● **Uplands**
Italy has two major mountain ranges, the Alps to the north of the country and the Apennines, which run down the center of the peninsula. In addition the country has a variety of upland landscapes, such as the sub-Apennines and the Abruzzi Mountains

● **Coastal plains**
The coastal areas of eastern Italy are largely fertile plains and there are more plains around the instep of Italy's "heel."

THE TERRAIN

Geographers divide Italy's terrain into eight land areas: the Alps, the Po Valley, the Adriatic Plain, the Apennines, Puglia (Apulia) and the Southeastern Plains, the Western Uplands, and the islands of Sicily and Sardinia.

The Alps

The Alps, the highest mountain range in Europe, curve across the top of Italy. They form the country's frontiers with its neighbors—France, Switzerland, Austria, and Slovenia. Just over the French border is Mont Blanc, the highest mountain in Europe at 15,771 feet (4,807m). The peaks of these ancient mountains are rocky and snowcapped all year. There are more than 1,000 glaciers, left from the last Ice Age.

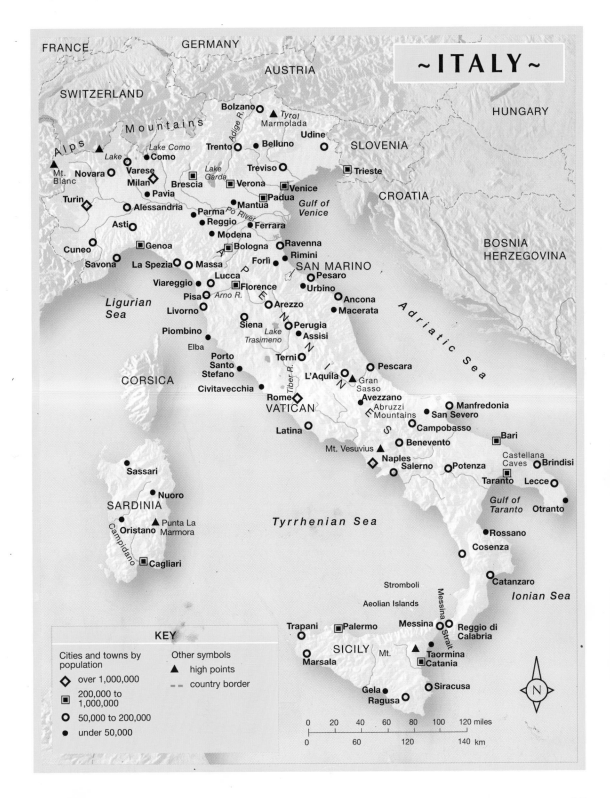

~ITALY~

FRANCE
GERMANY
AUSTRIA
SWITZERLAND
HUNGARY

Mountains
Bolzano
▲ Tyrol
Marmolada
Alps
Lake Como
Udine
SLOVENIA
Lake
Trento
Belluno
▲ Mt.
Blanc
Novara
Varese
Como
Treviso
Trieste
Milan
Brescia
Lake Garda
Verona
Venice
CROATIA
Pavia
Padua
Turin
Alessandria
Mantua
Po River
Gulf of
Venice
Asti
Parma
Ferrara
Reggio
Cuneo
Modena
BOSNIA
HERZEGOVINA
Savona
Genoa
Bologna
Ravenna
La Spezia
Massa
Forlì
Rimini
Viareggio
Lucca
SAN MARINO
Pesaro
Ligurian
Sea
Pisa
Florence
Urbino
Arno R.
Arezzo
Ancona
Livorno
Macerata
Piombino
Siena
Perugia
Adriatic Sea
Elba
Lake
Trasimeno
Assisi
Porto
Santo
Stefano
Terni
Tiber R.
Pescara
CORSICA
Civitavecchia
L'Aquila
Gran
Sasso
Rome
Avezzano
Manfredonia
VATICAN
Abruzzi
Mountains
San Severo
Latina
Campobasso
Bari
Benevento
Castellana
Caves
Brindisi
Sassari
Mt. Vesuvius
Naples
Salerno
Potenza
Taranto
Lecce
Nuoro
SARDINIA
Gulf of
Taranto
Otranto
Oristano
Punta La
Marmora
Campidano
Tyrrhenian Sea
Rossano
Cagliari
Cosenza
Stromboli
Catanzaro
Aeolian Islands
Ionian Sea
Messina Strait
Trapani
Palermo
Messina
Reggio di
Calabria
SICILY
Mt.
Taormina
Marsala
Catania
Gela
Siracusa
Ragusa
N

KEY

Cities and towns by population

Other symbols

◇ over 1,000,000
■ 200,000 to 1,000,000
◎ 50,000 to 200,000
● under 50,000

▲ high points
-- country border

| 0 | 20 | 40 | 60 | 80 | 100 | 120 miles |

| 0 | | 60 | | 120 | | 140 km |

The Dolomites, which stretch across the northern region of Trentino-Alto Adige into the Veneto, are popular with hikers. The area contains many refuges, publicly maintained cabins, with minimal provisions, where hikers can take shelter from the weather.

Lower down the mountains, there are forests of beech, oak, and chestnut, as well as conifer. Road and railroad tunnels have been dug through the rock to allow traffic and trains to reach other countries, even in winter weather.

At the northeastern end of the Alps, the mountains are formed of limestone rocks called "dolomites," which give the massif its name, the Dolomites. The highest point in the Dolomites is the Marmolada, which rises to 10,964 feet (3,342 m). The limestone has been eroded to make a landscape of steep, jagged rocks shaped like towers and domes. These contrast with the lower slopes, which curve gently and are covered with green pastures, pine trees, and crops.

The Po Valley and the Adriatic Plain

Italy's longest river is the Po. It rises in the northwest, in the Alps, near the border with France, and runs east to the Adriatic Sea. The river flows for 405 miles (652 km) through a flat plain called the Po Valley. Sometimes the Po floods, although a system of dikes helps to control this. Italy's second-longest river, the Adige, flows 255 miles (410 km) also through the Po Valley. It rises in the Dolomites and flows down to a delta south of the city of Venice.

The city of Turin is the capital of the wealthy Piedmont region. It is also home to the Fiat automobile company.

More than 60 percent of all the lowland in Italy is in the Po Valley. Made up of the river's rich silt, this area has the best farmland in Italy. The area is the most densely populated part of the country, with two large cities—Milan and Turin. Industrial zones and suburbs lie around the cities.

The Adriatic Plain is a small plain to the east of the city of Venice. The eastern half—the Carso Plateau—borders on Slovenia. The land here is very poor.

The Apennines

The Apennines, a major range of mountains, extend nearly the whole length of Italy, making a long zigzag about 620 miles (1,000 km) down the peninsula. In the north at Genoa, the Apennines first follow the west coast, then reach across to the east coast at Pesaro. Farther south, the Apennines veer westward again toward the Mediterranean and continue from Naples down to the Messina Strait.

The Apennines stretch to 120 miles (193 km) at their widest point in central Italy. The only Apennine glacier, Calderone, in the rugged Gran Sasso area, is the southernmost glacier in Europe.

The massif of the Gran Sasso (whose name means literally "large rock") contains the highest of the Apennine peaks. These tower over the regions of Abruzzo, Le Marche, and eastern Lazio.

The southern end of the Apennines is a volcanic area. The most famous volcano is Mount Vesuvius—3,891 feet (1,185 m) high—near Naples. Gases often force their way up through the craters. There have been devastating eruptions in the past, and there could be others at any time. Sometimes flows of glowing lava are pushed out of the volcanoes, destroying buildings or crops.

The Tuscan countryside is characterized by rolling hills, covered in vineyards. The Tuscan region is Italy's most important wine producer, notably for the wines of the Chianti, the area that lies between Florence and Siena.

Western Uplands and Plains

This area stretches along the Tyrrhenian Sea from just south of Genoa in the northwest right down to Rome and past Naples along the central western coast. It is densely populated, especially around the great urban centers of Rome and Naples.

The land here is very fertile, second only to the Po Valley for its quantity of agricultural produce. In the north, grain crops are grown and cattle are raised. The land here is excellent for fruit and vegetable farming. There are also many vineyards in the region. As land for agriculture is precious, marshland was drained during the 1930s in the Maremma of southern Tuscany and also in Agro Pontino in Lazio.

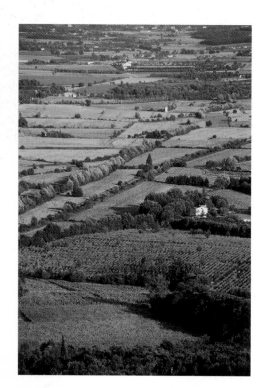

In central Italy, the Arno River—150 miles (241 km) long—rises in the Apennines and flows west. It passes through the cities of Florence and Pisa before reaching the Ligurian Sea. The Tiber, at 252 miles (405 km) Italy's third-longest river—flows through the capital, Rome. In 1966 many rivers in central Italy burst their banks and there was widespread flooding. Florence was submerged as the waters of the Arno rose. Buildings and artworks were damaged, some beyond repair. In the city, signs on walls show high-water marks (*see* p. 31).

Puglia and the Southeastern Plains

Most of Puglia, down in the "heel" of Italy, comprises a series of flat, limestone plateaus, with some higher ground in the Gargano Peninsula. The largest plain area is the Tavoliere Plain. The Castellana Caves are a series of limestone caves, with spectacular stalactites and stalagmites.

Sicily and Sardinia

The largest island in the Mediterranean, Sicily covers 10,027 square miles (25,709 sq. km). It is a triangle shape and, in ancient times, was even called *Trinakria*, the Greek word for "triangle." The highest point is Mount Etna, an active volcano, which rises to 10,959 feet (3,340 m). An earthquake destroyed Messina on the north of the island in 1908, and in 1968 another earthquake caused damage to the west of the island. Etna's last major eruption was in 1992, when a lava flow stopped just short of the town of Zafferana Etnea.

Mount Etna looms over the Sicilian coast south of Taormina. It is Europe's biggest volcano and one of the largest in the world.

Sardinia, the second largest Mediterranean island, covers 9,300 square miles (24,089 sq km), and is largely mountainous. About 1.6 million people live on the island. Because of the remoteness of the island's interior, the people here have remained relatively distinct and they are known throughout Italy for their black hair and distinctive looks. The island has two mountain ranges separated by the long plain of Campidano, which cuts a diagonal southeast across the island. Just south of the center of the island is the Gennargentu Range. The highest point is the Punta La Marmora, which is 6,017 feet (1,834 m).

VALLE D'AOSTA

TRENTINO-ALTO ADIGE

FRIULI-VENEZIA GIULIA

LOMBARDY

VENETO

PIEDMONT

EMILIA-ROMAGNA

LIGURIA

TUSCANY

LE MARCHE

UMBRIA

ABRUZZO

LAZIO

MOLISE

PUGLIA

CAMPANIA

BASILICATA

SARDINIA

CALABRIA

SICILY

THE REGIONS OF ITALY

Italy is divided into 20 regions, which are then further subdivided into a number of provinces. Each of the regions has a strong local character and usually its own dialect. The map shows the 20 regions, which are listed on the left with their capitals. These regional capitals are indicated on the map with a dot.

ABRUZZO L'Aquila
BASILICATA Potenza
CALABRIA Catanzaro
CAMPANIA Naples
EMILIA-ROMAGNA Bologna
FRIULI-VENEZIA GIULIA Trieste
LAZIO Rome
LIGURIA Genoa
LOMBARDY Milan
LE MARCHE Ancona
MOLISE Campobasso
PIEDMONT Turin
PUGLIA Bari
SARDINIA Cagliari
SICILY Palermo
TRENTINO-ALTO ADIGE Trento
TUSCANY Florence
UMBRIA Perugia
VALLE D'AOSTA Aosta
VENETO Venice

The region of Piedmont, whose name comes from the French for "foot of the mountain," was French speaking until the end of the 19th century. Although it was ruled by France for many years, it played a leading role in the unification of Italy.

THE REGIONS

Italy is divided into 20 administrative regions, each with its own regional capital. The largest region is the southern island of Sicily; the smallest is Valle d'Aosta ("Valley of Aosta") in the northwest. Many of the regional boundaries are based on the historic areas into which Italy was divided before 1861.

There are still differences between the regions, not just in landscape and climate, but also in food, customs, language, and lifestyles. People in Italy are very attached to the place that they come from. Even when they move away, they still feel that their birthplace or region is very important.

Five of the regions—Sicily, Sardinia, Valle d'Aosta, Trentino-Alto Adige, and Friuli-Venezia Giulia—have a special status because they are islands or because they border other countries. Valle d'Aosta is near France, while Trentino-Alto Adige and Friuli-Venezia-Giulia border on Austria and Slovenia respectively.

At regional level, voters elect a regional council. In turn, the members of the regional council elect an executive and its president as the regional government. Each region is subdivided into provinces. There are 94 provinces in total. In turn, a province is divided into *comuni*. A *comune* could be a village, a small town, or a city. There are 8,091 *comuni* in Italy. Each *comune* has an elected mayor and a council. They look after local matters such as public transportation, garbage collection, and street lighting.

The Alpine village of Dolonne sits right on the border with France in the shadow of Mont Blanc.

The North

The north is traditionally the wealthiest part of Italy and is home to much of the country's industry and most fertile land. In the northwest corner of Italy are four regions: Valle d'Aosta, Piedmont, Liguria, and Lombardy. Valle d'Aosta is Italy's smallest region. The highest Alpine peaks lie within the region, and many mountain towns serve as ski resorts, attracting thousands of tourists in winter.

Lying partly in the Alps but mostly in the Po Valley, Piedmont is Italy's second-largest region. The Po River flows through the capital, Turin. Turin is a bustling manufacturing center and home of the Italian automobile industry. Southeast of Turin, in the Monferrato Hills, famous wines are made around Asti. Near Alba in the south of Piedmont, trained dogs hunt for aromatic white truffles from the soil.

Liguria occupies a small strip of territory where the Alps plunge into the sea. The regional capital is the ancient city of Genoa. The sunny Ligurian coast, with its elegant resorts and picturesque fishing villages, attracts many visitors. To the east of Piedmont is the wealthy region of Lombardy. This sprawling region is Italy's center for industry, banking, and fashion. To the north, Lakes Maggiore and Como are popular destinations for summer trips out of the regional capital Milan.

The northeast corner of Italy has three regions: Trentino-Alto Adige, Friuli-Venezia Giulia, and the Veneto. The Veneto stretches from Lake Garda east to the regional capital, Venice. Like many other northern regions, Veneto is a wealthy area, with a thriving industrial sector, much of it centered around Venice's industrial suburb of Mestre. There are many old towns and cities in the Veneto, including Verona and Padua. Out in the countryside are handsome villas, once the homes of the powerful and wealthy who liked to spend their summers away from the sweltering heat of the busy cities.

North of Veneto is Trentino-Alto Adige, which stretches north into the Dolomites. The region has two capitals, Trento and Bolzano, one for the Italian-speaking majority and one for the German-speaking minority. The regional assembly sits in each capital alternately. The Italian name Bolzano has a German equivalent—Bolzen. Many towns here have a German name and an Italian one. The region of Friuli-Venezia Giulia borders Slovenia and has a Slovenian-speaking minority. The capital, on the eastern edge of the region, is the seaport of Trieste.

Italians top a dish of pasta or risotto with finely grated Parmesan cheese. Real Parmesan cheese comes from the Emilia-Romagna region, especially around the city of Parma.

Lovelorn in Verona

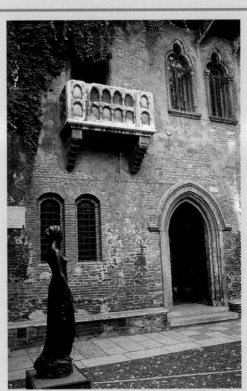

Romeo and Juliet, or *Giulietta e Romeo* as the Italians say, have made the city of Verona famous around the world. The couple were never real people but come from the dramatist William Shakespeare's reworking of a 15th-century story. Many visitors still come in search of the lovers. An old house in the city center is called Juliet's House, and people stand there and imagine the famous balcony scene, in which Juliet calls for her lover. Some people write grafitti on the walls.

Those who cannot visit Verona sometimes write letters to the city about their romantic problems. Most of the letters come from the United States, France, Italy, China, and Poland. A team of paid staff and volunteers takes turns answering the letters in a variety of languages, signing them "Juliet" or "Juliet's secretary." A psychologist advises on the more complicated situations. Each year there is even a prize for the best letter.

Central Italy

The center of Italy comprises seven regions: Emilia-Romagna, Tuscany, Umbria, Le Marche, Lazio, Abruzzo, and Molise. The geographical center of the Italian peninsula is at Rieti in Lazio.

Emilia-Romagna is the northernmost of the central Italian regions. It is a region of fertile plains famous for its agricultural products, including wheat, corn, and sugar beet, as well as dairy products. It takes part of its name from the Via Emilia, an ancient Roman road that crossed the Po Plain from Piacenza southeast to Rimini on the coast. The regional capital is Bologna, famous for its arcaded streets, its large university, and its rich, tasty cuisine. Bologna is also an industrial center with steel, engineering, and food-processing plants.

Tuscany shares a long regional border with Emilia-Romagna. Its capital is the beautiful, historic city of Florence. Tuscany and its southern neighbor, Umbria, have landscapes of rounded green hills. In addition to Florence, the region has many historic towns, including Siena, Pisa, Arezzo, and Lucca, which attract visitors from all over the world. The land along the Arno River

Politically, central Italy was the base of support for the Communist Party. The wealthy region of Emilia-Romagna is now controlled by the PDS, the reformed version of the Communist Party.

Bologna is famous for its medieval towers, which were originally built as lookouts. Wealthy landowners later tried to outdo each other with the height of the buildings.

is fertile, producing wheat and corn, as well as olives and grapes for wine. Prato, near Florence, is one of the main centers for textile production in the country.

Off the coast of Tuscany is the Tuscan Archipelago. The largest island in this group is Elba. Largely mountainous, the island depends on tourism and iron-ore mining, which has taken place there since ancient times.

The region of Umbria south of Tuscany has no coastline. It is famous for its old hilltop towns, including Assisi, Gubbio, and Spoleto. The capital, Perugia, also sits high on a hill and was home to an ancient people known as the Etruscans (*see* pp. 48–49), who once rivaled the Romans. The town of Assisi also attracts millions of visitors every year. Saint Francis, who founded the religious order of Franciscan monks, was born in Assisi in 1182 and spent his life there. In 1998, its beautiful old basilica was badly damaged in an earthquake and priceless frescoes were lost.

The hilly, secluded region of Le Marche ("the Marches") lies on the eastern side of the Apennines. The regional capital, Ancona, is an ancient seaport.

The capital of Italy, Rome, lies in the Lazio region. On hot summer weekends, Romans head west to the beach at Ostia, which was a port in ancient Roman times. Today, the only modern port along Lazio's long, sandy coastline is at Civitavecchia. To the south of Rome are the Alban Hills, where the pope has his summer home at Castel Gandolfo. Close to the sea and separated from it by low sandy hills are the Pontine Marshes. For a long time, this was an area of unhealthy swamps, but in the 20th century much of the area was drained and new towns were built.

Abruzzo and Molise are both mountainous, remote regions on the eastern side of the Apennines. Until 1963,

At the Lake

Not far from Perugia is Lake Trasimeno. It is the largest lake in south and central Italy, covering 50 square miles (128 sq. km). It is well known for a fierce battle fought on its northern shores in 217 B.C. Hannibal of Carthage and his army defeated the Romans, killing 16,000 soldiers. Today, visitors come to the lake for more peaceful pursuits. The waters of the lake are only 23-feet (7-m) deep and therefore remain relatively warm.

The region of Lazio is also known as Latium. This region was traditionally ruled by the great families of Rome and in its countryside many of their magnificent villas can still be seen.

Molise was a part of Abruzzo. The landscape of Abruzzo is wild, with rugged mountains. L'Aquila, the capital, is an old medieval town. Abruzzo is often called the "Park Region" because 30 percent of its land is protected by environmental laws. The highest Apennine peak is found in the Abruzzo—the Gran Corno, at 9,560 feet (2,914 m).

The South

The south of Italy is also known as the *Mezzogiorno*, which means "midday" as well as "south," evoking images of its dazzling, sun-drenched landscapes. Traditionally, the south has been one of the poorest areas of Italy, with little industry and poor farmland. The area also has a reputation for lawlessness and is the homeland of the mafia, a criminal fraternity (*see* p. 74). The four regions of Campania, Puglia, Basilicata, and Calabria are very beautiful, famous for their high, craggy mountains, fragrant lemon orchards, and deep-blue coastal waters.

The capital of Campania is Naples, the largest city and home to the main industrial zone in the south. Curving along the Bay of Naples, the region includes the

Capital of the Campania region, Naples is a loud, chaotic, bustling city with a successful textiles industry and a thriving black market. The city is home to over a million people.

Under the Volcano

The looming outline of Mount Vesuvius and its plumes of smoke are a familiar sight to the people of Naples. It might seem strange that people would want to live so close to an active volcano. The main reason why people first founded villages near Vesuvius is the richness of the soil. Over time, as lava solidifies and breaks down, it becomes very fertile soil.

People grow a great range of crops in the rich, black soil that surrounds the lower slopes of the crater. There are orange and lemon groves and vineyards. Lacryma Christi (literally the "tears of Christ"), a famous white wine, is produced from grapes grown near Vesuvius. The wine label shows a picture of the volcano.

Volcanologists—scientists who study volcanoes—believe that Vesuvius could be due for another major eruption like that which destroyed the city of Pompeii. They monitor the behavior of the volcano carefully, trying to detect signs of any impending eruption.

ancient Roman town of Pompeii. When the volcano Vesuvius erupted in A.D. 79, Pompeii was covered by rocks and ash. The virtually intact city was only rediscovered and excavated centuries later. Splendid villas and gardens were uncovered, together with brightly colored frescoes and other art treasures. The petrified bodies of the city's inhabitants were found lying just where they died, often curled up on the ground as they sought to protect themselves from the burning ash and poisonous fumes. Today the Campania coast is famous as a luxury vacation destination and is dotted with scenic resorts, such as those along the Amalfi coast and the towns of Positano and Sorrento.

On the Adriatic coast, the region of Puglia forms the "heel" of Italy. The capital is the port city of Bari, which is the second-largest city of the south. It is a thriving center of new technology industries and hosts an important trade fair every September. Basilicata, between Puglia and Campania, has a short coast on the Tyrrhenian Sea and another, longer one on the Ionian Sea. Some of the land is poor because trees have been

Carlo Levi, a famous Italian author who was exiled to a remote region of Basilicata by the Nazis, described his experiences in *Christ Stopped at Eboli*. Published in 1945, it described the bleak nature of life in southern Italy at the time.

cut down and valuable soils have been lost through erosion. Potenza, the capital, is in the center of the region.

In Matera, there are stone houses built around caves in the ravines that cut across the town. Calabria is the mountainous "toe" of Italy, which pokes out between the Tyrrhenian and the Ionian Seas. It has more fertile land than Basilicata, and a few towns with a little industry, including Catanzaro, the regional capital. Just north of the tip of Calabria is Aspromonte, a rugged massif. From the top, there are views across the Messina Strait to Sicily.

Greek Temples

Just outside the Sicilian town of Agrigento stands a group of Greek temples unique outside of Greece itself. The town was founded in 581 B.C. by Greek colonists and the temples were mostly built in the fifth century B.C., though the oldest, the Temple of Hercules, was begun at the end of the sixth century B.C. The most complete is the Temple of Concorde with its sacrificial altar, which survives largely intact because the temple was converted into a church in the sixth century A.D.

Sicily

Sicily has a complex history. Waves of different people—Phoenicians, Greeks, Romans, Arabs, Normans, and Spanish—have occupied it and settled there over the centuries. These peoples left behind a rich variety of monuments, including temples, mosques, churches, castles, and palaces.

The population of Sicily is 5.1 million. The capital is the ancient city of Palermo in the west, but its commercial center is on the east coast at Catania. An oil refinery in the east handles crude oil extracted offshore near Gela and Ragusa. There are also petrochemical plants nearby.

Many Sicilians still have a close connection with the land. Around 40 percent of the population still work in agriculture. The main agricultural products are wheat, grown in the inland plains, and citrus fruits and grapes from the coastal zones.

The influence of the mafia (*see* p. 74) in many aspects of life, including business, is still very strong in Sicily. Many ordinary people want to take back power from organized crime and to get rid of corruption and improve everyone's standard of living. There is also a political movement *La Rete* which campaigns against the mafia.

Off the north coast of Sicily are the Aeolian, or Lipari, Islands. In ancient times, people thought of the islands as the home of the winds. This volcanic archipelago of seven islands includes the active volcano of Stromboli. Lava flows often erupt and drop dramatically from the side of the volcano into the sea. At night, the brilliant, fiery glow of the lava can be seen for miles around.

Sardinia

Like Sicily, the island of Sardinia has been settled by many different people. Scattered across the island are thousands of cone-shaped houses, left by the first people, the Nuraghi, who came here in around 2000 B.C.

For many years, Sardinia was relatively isolated, linked only to the Italian mainland by ferry. Perhaps for this reason, it managed to preserve its rich folk traditions, many of which date back hundreds of years. Every May, Sardinians dressed in traditional costumes take part in colorful processions.

The island's beautiful, rocky coastline now attracts many visitors. The first large-scale tourist development was the Costa Smeralda in the north of the island. Modern airports at Cagliari, Alghero, and Sassari bring visitors in by air.

Fishing is a major industry in Sardinia and the local cuisine reflects it, with local dishes of grilled lobster, fish stews, and bottarga, a type of caviar made from mullet eggs.

CLIMATE

Italy is in a temperate zone, which means that it is generally neither extremely hot nor cold. However, the farther south you go, the hotter and drier the country becomes. The mountains and the sea also influence the climate. For example, the west coast is usually warmer and wetter than the east.

In the Alps, the highest mountain peaks are covered in snow all year round. The snow line starts at 10,200 feet (3,108 m) in Valle d'Aosta and as low as 8,350 feet (2,545m) on the eastern side of the Alps. The Alps form a barrier against the cold winter weather of northern Europe, so winters around Lakes Garda, Como, and Maggiore are generally mild. In January, the nearby city of Milan has an average minimum temperature of 35°F (1°C), compared to 39°F (4°C) around Garda. The Ligurian Sea coast also has a mild winter because it is protected by the Alps and the Apennines. A little farther south in the Po Valley area, however, winters are cold and frosty and summers are hot and humid. Rain falls mainly in spring and fall. Snowfall is a possibility in the regions of Lombardy and Emilia-Romagna.

Central and southern Italy have a Mediterranean climate. Summers are long, hot, and dry. In Tuscany, they last three-and-a-half to four months; in Calabria summer

Midsummer temperatures are fairly uniform throughout the Italian peninsula. In winter the central region of the Po Valley and the areas around Italy's northern fringes frequently have temperatures below freezing, while in the south they barely drop below 50°F (10°C).

AVERAGE RAINFALL AND TEMPERATURE

Milan — in/cm: 16/40, 12/30, 8/20, 4/10, 0 — °F/°C: 77/25, 68/20, 59/15, 50/10, 41/5, 32/0 — Temperature, Rainfall — J F M A M J J A S O N D

Naples — in/cm: 16/40, 12/30, 8/20, 4/10, 0 — °F/°C: 77/25, 68/20, 59/15, 50/10, 41/5, 32/0 — Temperature, Rainfall — J F M A M J J A S O N D

Florence Floods 1966

The floods in Florence in November 1966 killed several people and caused huge amounts of damage to buildings and artworks. Here Professor Umberto Baldini, head of the Florence Restoration Board, describes his experience:

"...I rushed over to the restoration center but luckily there was no sign of any water there, so I went immediately on to the Uffizi; when I arrived I saw that the water had already nearly reached the height of a trolley bus. The water was nearly a meter and a half deep in Piazza Duomo and the situation was already serious in Piazza della Signoria as well. I managed to get inside the Uffizi but the water was already up to my waist.

Inside the Uffizi we tried to remove as many paintings as we could to safety; these included works by Giotto, Tiepolo, Mantegna, as well as the Virgin *by Filippo Lippi. We also managed to lift the* Coronation of the Virgin *by Botticelli high enough to prevent the water from touching, because it was too big to go through the door.*

Once we had got the paintings to safety we headed for the Vasari Corridor above the Ponte Vecchio to try to save the paintings that were in danger there. The bridge shuddered and we thought it was going to fall down. We managed to remove the paintings and immediately returned to the Uffizi from where we were able to see the fury of the Arno from the upstairs windows. We could see that the Ponte Vecchio was likely to fall down at any minute. Then it was given a violent blow by a lorry that had been carried away by the terrifying floodwaters, which caused the walls to collapse like a pack of cards. This terrible impact made an enormous hole in the bridge but also created a path for the floodwaters. That blow was what saved the Ponte Vecchio.

It was 3:30 in the morning when the waters finally went down and the city was left in total darkness."

lasts five months and winters there are mild. Calabria and Sicily are surrounded by sea, so they have higher temperatures than the areas farther north, together with low rainfall. The average minimum January temperature in Palermo in Sicily is 44°F (8°C). In July and August, the temperature rises to 86°F (30°C). Because it is farther west, Sardinia's climate is influenced somewhat by the Atlantic. It can also get the hot sirocco wind blowing up from Africa or the cold mistral wind from the northwest.

WILDLIFE AND VEGETATION

Italy's animals and plants are as varied as its landscapes. However, because large areas of Italy are farmed or settled, the country's most interesting wildlife lies in remote places such as mountains or in coastal waters. In the Alps live species that are well adapted to the cold climate. The coats of stoats and Alpine rabbits as well as the feathers of mountain partridge turn white to match the winter snow, while other animals, such as the marmot, hibernate (sleep through the winter) to conserve their energy and keep warm.

The chamois is one of the species that is protected in the Alps region. Italy's large hunting community is a real threat to wildlife, particularly in the north of the country.

In the Gran Paradiso National Park in the Alps, ibex are protected and can roam freely. These mountain goats have large horns that curve backward. In the Central Alps, there are chamois, a type of goat antelope, with straight horns that point up and back. Alpine birds include black grouse and the rare golden eagle. Other mountain animals such as lynx, stoats, brown bears, and wolves are now rare. Brown bears are protected, and more often found in the wilder parts of Abruzzo. Remote areas of Sardinia are home to fallow deer, mouflon sheep, and wild boar.

In the seas off Italy, especially farther south, are large numbers of white sharks, bluefin tuna, and swordfish. In the warmer southern seas, there are also red coral and sponge, a marine animal with a fibrous skeleton.

Centuries ago, Italy was covered with forests. As towns and cities were built, many of these disappeared. The Umbra Forest in the Gargano Peninsula, in Puglia, is one of the last of these original forests in Italy, with beeches and oaks. There are also beechwoods in Calabria, as well as silver fir and pine forests in Abruzzo.

Where these ancient forests have disappeared in the Mediterranean parts of the Apennines low scrub called *macchia* has grown up. *Macchia* includes wild olives, oleander, laurel, myrtle, holm oaks, cork oaks, and cluster pines. This is now considered perhaps the most characteristic vegetation of mainland Italy. Cypresses and olive trees are a typical part of the landscape in sunny Mediterranean regions. Cork oaks have a thick layer under the bark, which is often used for making bottle corks and other cork products. In the mountain meadowlands of Calabria and Basilicata can be found vetch, bent grass, and white asphodel. By contrast, the areas of the Po Valley contain almost nothing of the original forests, because they have been converted completely into farmland.

The tall, slim forms of cypress trees are a characteristic of the Italian landscape, particularly in the central regions of Umbria and Tuscany.

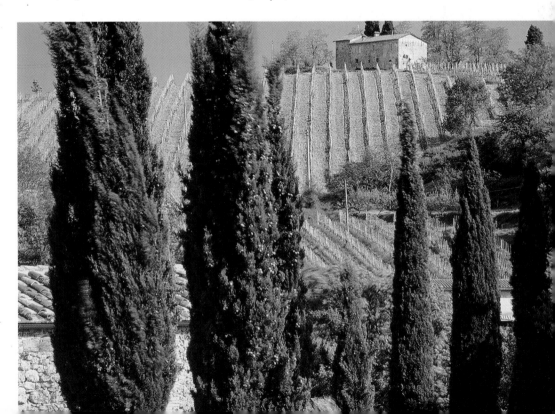

Italy's National Parks

To protect Italy's rare or endangered species of wildlife, trees, and plants, there are 19 national parks, with five more planned. Altogether, they will cover an area equivalent to 5 percent of Italy's land area. The two largest parks are in the Alps: Stelvio (521 square miles; 1,350 sq. km) and Gran Paradiso (270 square miles; 700 sq. km). The smallest is on Cape Circeo, along the coast south of Rome. The areas protected are very varied, including part of the Alps, the volcano Vesuvius, coastal areas, and even whole islands and archipelagoes. There are also many regional parks throughout the country.

VALGRANDE STELVIO

GRAN PARADISO

DOLOMITI BELLUNESI

M. FALTERONA-CAMPIGNA

FORÉSTE CASENTINESI

MONTI SIBILLINI

ARCHIPELAGO TOSCANO

GRAN SASSO

MAIELLA

ISOLA DELL'ASINARA

GARGANO

ABRUZZO

CIRCEO

VESUVIO

GOLFO DI OROSEI-MONTI DEL GENNARGENTU

CILENTO E VALLO DI DIANO

POLLINO

CALABRIA

Rural Life

As with Italy's industry, farms in Italy are usually family concerns, a fact that is reflected in the small size of most holdings, although there are large farmlands in the Po Valley. There wheat and corn are the most common crops. In remoter regions, farming concentrates on wine-making and livestock farming. In the south, the larger farms are worked by people who live in nearby towns. In Sicily the population is clustered around "peasant cities" which reflect the historical structure of Sicilian society.

CITIES

Italy is unusual in not being dominated by any one city. Each region has its own capital and a strong sense of identity. This reflects the country's past, when areas such as Naples and Sicily, or city-states, such as Florence, Pisa, and Venice, were separate states. In terms of population, the largest cities are Rome, Milan, Naples, and Turin, all with populations over one million; in many respects, however, the smaller cities are equally important.

Rome

Rome is one of the world's great historical cities. It enjoyed two periods of importance. In ancient times, it was the center of a civilization and a mighty empire that spread across Europe, west Asia, and north Africa. Later, the city was the most important center for Christianity and, as such, its power and influence are still felt across the globe. Because of its age-old importance, Rome is often referred to as the "Eternal City."

The city center is a fascinating mixture of ancient monuments and bustling city life and noisy traffic. The original center spreads over seven hills: the Palatine, Aventine, Capitoline, Quirinale, Viminale, Esquiline, and Celian.

From the top of the Capitoline Hill the remains of the Forum can be seen (*see* p. 46). This was the place where the people of ancient Rome came to worship, settle political issues, do business, or simply socialize. On a walk through the grassy site a visitor can see what is left of temples and other public buildings. Other ancient monuments—triumphal arches, public baths, temples, villas—can also be seen in the city. Outside the center are the catacombs, the underground tombs of the early Christians.

The Spanish Steps, which lead up to the church of Trinità dei Monti—seen here in the distance—are one of the main tourist attractions of Rome. They run down to the Piazza di Spagna (Spanish Square), which took its name from the main building there, the Spanish Embassy.

The ancient city of Rome was built around the seven hills. The center of the modern city is largely built on the right bank of the Tiber, with the Vatican on the left. To the south of the current city lie the remains of the Forum, the Colosseum and, farther south, the remains of the giant baths complexes. The city's principal street is the narrow thoroughfare of the Via del Corso.

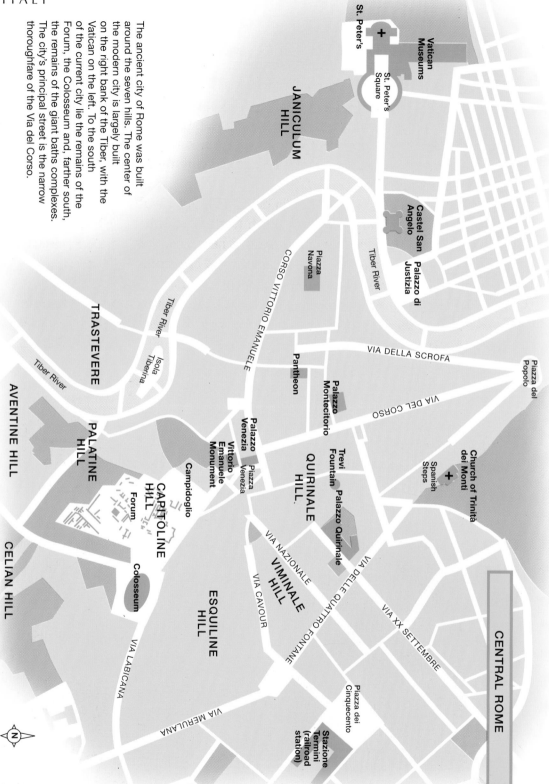

CENTRAL ROME

St. Peter's

Vatican Museums

St. Peter's Square

Castel San Angelo

Palazzo di Justizia

JANICULUM HILL

Tiber River

Piazza Navona

CORSO VITTORIO EMANUELE

Piazza del Popolo

VIA DELLA SCROFA

Pantheon

VIA DEL CORSO

Palazzo Montecitorio

Church of Trinità dei Monti

Spanish Steps

Trevi Fountain

Palazzo Venezia

Piazza Venezia

QUIRINALE HILL

Palazzo Quirinale

TRASTEVERE

Tiber River

Isola Tiberina

Vittorio Emanuele Monument

Campidoglio

CAPITOLINE HILL

Forum

VIA NAZIONALE

VIA DELLE QUATTRO FONTANE

VIA XX SETTEMBRE

PALATINE HILL

AVENTINE HILL

Colosseum

VIMINALE HILL

VIA CAVOUR

ESQUILINE HILL

CELIAN HILL

VIA LABICANA

VIA MERULANA

Piazza dei Cinquecento

Stazione Termini (railroad station)

N

On top of the Capitoline Hill is the Campidoglio, an elegant Renaissance square designed by Michelangelo in 1536. Around the square are a 13th-century church and the Capitoline Museums, housing one of the great collections of Roman sculpture. At the foot of the Capitoline, in Piazza Venezia, stands the Palazzo Venezia, once the Venetian Embassy and later the center of Mussolini's Fascist government (*see* p. 71).

From the Piazza Venezia, the Via del Corso, lined with fashionable shops and cafés, runs north to the Piazza del Popolo, one of the city's largest squares. The piazza was once a gateway to the city and the gate can still be seen. In the center of the piazza is an ancient Egyptian obelisk.

The Piazza Navona, a pleasant square of 18th-century houses, has at its center the Fountain of the Four Rivers, a Baroque structure by Gian Lorenzo Bernini (1598–1680).

Rome's ornate Monument to Victor Emmanuel II was built in honor of Italy's first king after unification. The Romans call it "the typewriter" because of its shape, but visiting GIs called it "the wedding cake" because its white marble never discolors.

The Colosseum

The largest Roman buildings were great feats of engineering. The first-century Colosseum still stands near the Forum. This vast amphitheater, which took 12 years to build, measures 1,729 feet (527m) in circumference and stands 187 feet (57m) high. Four levels of seating for 80,000 spectators were supported by a structure of vaults and arches, hidden behind a simple, curving outside wall. A linen awning was stretched across the top to protect spectators from the sun or the rain. The arena could be flooded for naval and aquatic displays. People went to watch gladiators fight each other or wild animals, races, and naval battles.

The Rome Subway

The Roman subway has two intersecting lines that meet at the main railroad station, Termini.

In the 18th century the piazza would be flooded and Roman aristocrats would float around in horse-drawn boats. Another Baroque fountain is a famous landmark in Rome. The Trevi Fountain is an elaborate monument created by Nicol Salvi in 1762. It has a large sculpture of a sea god in a chariot drawn by two seahorses. There is a custom that, standing with your back to the fountain, you throw in two coins. The first coin is so that you will come back to Rome, the second is to have a wish granted.

On the opposite side of Via del Corso stands the Pantheon. Previously a Roman temple, in A.D. 609 it was consecrated as a church. The building is one of the masterpieces of Roman architecture. Its diameter, at 164 feet (43 m), is exactly the same as its height—a perfect sphere would fit inside it, indicating the building's original role as a temple to the planetary gods. It is covered by a vast dome, supported only by the struts that run down through the concrete walls. The building was to have a major influence on European architecture. Its dome was made possible by the use of concrete mixed with rubble, which created a solid mass that could be stretched over a large area, thus creating a vast interior uninterrupted by supports. A small-scale example of a building influenced by the Pantheon is the university library at Charlottesville in Virginia—although the domes of the Panthéon in Paris, St. Peter's in Rome, and St. Paul's in London are more widely known.

When Romans go out for an evening, they may visit areas like Trastevere on the west bank of the Tiber, which has many restaurants and cafés, or Testaccio to the south, which is popular with a younger crowd and has lively discos and clubs. Central Rome is served by an extensive metro and light railroad system, although new lines have been halted by the discovery of archaeological remains.

The Vatican

The Vatican City, from which the Roman Catholic church is governed, occupies 109 acres (44 hectares) within the city of Rome. At Easter, up to 300,000 worshipers gather outside St. Peter's to hear the pope give his blessing. As they gather in St. Peter's Square, they are surrounded by the magnificent colonnade created by Gian Lorenzo Bernini between 1656 and 1667. Two semicircles, made up of four rows of colossal columns, curve in toward the façade of St. Peter's Basilica. The basilica stands on the site where St. Peter was allegedly buried after he was martyred. It was based on a plan conceived in the 15th century, but the actual building was mostly completed in the 16th and 17th centuries and involved some of the greatest architects of the Renaissance.

Inside the Vatican buildings are masterpieces painted by Raphael and Michelangelo. Michelangelo spent four years painting the ceiling of the Sistine Chapel, where cardinals meet to elect the pope. The chapel is named after Pope Sixtus IV, for whom it was completed in 1481.

In addition to the church itself, the Vatican also houses a series of museums containing some of the greatest treasures in the Western world, including Renaissance painting, classical sculpture, and Etruscan, Greek, and Egyptian artifacts. Also enclosed within the Vatican City is the Castel San Angelo, a vast castle built by the Roman emperor Hadrian as his mausoleum and later used by the popes as a fortress in times of siege.

Florence

Of Florence's six central bridges, the Ponte Vecchio was the only one not to be mined when the Nazis attacked the city in 1944. Hitler gave direct instructions that the historic bridge was not to be damaged.

The cities of Florence and Venice are among the most popular places for tourists in the world, not just in Italy, because they have so many historic buildings and priceless art treasures. Both cities depend to a large extent on tourism, but the people who live there often feel the pressure of the millions of visitors who come every year.

Florence stands on the Arno River. The most famous bridge over the river is the Ponte Vecchio (the "old bridge"), a 14th-century structure lined with jewelry stores. Many of the buildings in the historic center of Florence were constructed during the Renaissance. They often have plain, regular façades with overhanging roofs that give shelter for passersby.

Walking north from the Arno, visitors pass the Uffizi Gallery, which the Florentine leader Cosimo the Great had built in the second half of the 16th century. It was originally an office building for work in the city government (its name means "offices"), but now it houses the greatest collection of Italian Renaissance art in the world. The paintings are arranged chronologically. There are works by 13th-century painters like Cimabue, Giotto, and Simone Martini. The most famous exhibits are the works of Renaissance painters. Two paintings by Sandro Botticelli (1445–1510) are well-known worldwide: his *Birth of Venus*

Built in 1345, the Ponte Vecchio's upper story contains the Vasari Corridor, which links the Palazzo Vecchio with the Palazzo Pitti.

CENTRAL FLORENCE

Station

Piazza della
Stazione

Central
Market

Piazza San
Lorenzo

Palazzo
Medici-
Riccardi

Piazza dell' Unita
Italiana

Santa Maria
Novella

VIA SANT' ANTONIO

VIA BUFALINI

Piazza Santa
Maria Novella

VIA DEI CERRETANI

Baptistery Duomo

VIA DEL PORCELLANA

VIA PALAZZUOLO

FOSSI

VIA BRUNELLESCHI

VIA DEI TOSSENGHI

VIA DEL PROCONSOLO

VIA DE'

VIA DE' TORNABUONI

Piazza della
Repubblica

VIA DEL CORSO

VIA DEI CALZAIUOLI

Piazza Carlo
Goldoni

VIA DELLA VIGNA NUOVA

Palazzo
Strozzi

VIA

DEI PANDOLFINI

Orsanmichele

Bargello

LUNGARNO CORSINI

Piazza Santa
Trinità

VIA DELLA CONDOTTA

VIA DELLE TERME

Piazza della
Signoria

N

BORGO SANTI APOSTOLI

Loggia di
Signoria

Palazzo
Vecchio

PONTE S. TRINITA

LUNGARNO ACCIAUOLI

Uffizi

VIA DI NINNA

Arno River

PONTE VECCHIO

and *Primavera* (Spring). In *Primavera* (*see* p. 97) the figure of Lorenzo the Magnificent (1449–1492) can be seen on the left, portrayed as the god Mercury with a bow and arrows. Lorenzo sponsored many artists. Works by Michelangelo, Raphael, and many other great painters are also on view in the Uffizi.

Past the Uffizi Gallery is the Piazza della Signoria, the main square of historic Florence. So many statues are dotted around that it is like an outdoor sculpture exhibition. There are copies of famous statues like

Florence is famous for its museums such as the Bargello (sculpture), the Uffizi (painting), and the palaces of its great families, such as the Medici and the Strozzi.

The tower of the Palazzo Vecchio, the ancient council building of Florence, seen from the roof of the cathedral. In the background is the fort of Belvedere.

Michelangelo's *David* (the original is in the city's Accademia museum) and Cellini's sculpture of the ancient Greek hero Perseus (the original is now in Florence's sculpture museum, the Bargello). The Palazzo Vecchio (or "Old Palace", also known as the Palazzo della Signoria) on the square was the seat of the city government, the *signoria*. Passing along Via dei Calzaiuoli you reach the Duomo (cathedral). The cathedral of Santa Maria del Fiore was begun in 1296, but took almost 150 years to finish. The exterior is covered in designs of pink, white, and green marble, topped by a soaring red-tiled dome. The dome was designed by Filippo Brunelleschi (1377–1446), who brought Renaissance ideas into architecture. There was no scaffolding suitable for building a domed roof over such a large building until Brunelleschi came up with the revolutionary idea of building up the dome in self-supporting, horizontal layers that did not need so much scaffolding. It is possible to climb the stone steps that wind around the dome to the top for a view out over Florence.

For everyday needs there is a large, covered market, the *Mercato Centrale*, where food is sold. The streets nearby are lined with open-air stalls selling clothes, leather goods, and jewelry, all of which are important industries in Florence. Fashion and shoe shops are clustered along Via dei Calzaiuoli and Via de' Tornabuoni.

Venice

With a population of only 75,000 people, Venice has 23 million tourist visitors a year. They come out across the lagoon from the mainland by car, tour bus, or train, to see an extraordinary city. It was originally built up on stakes driven into mudbanks, which then formed the islands that we know today. The city has canals instead of roads and streets. Venetians do not go to work by car, they walk or take a *vaporetto* (waterbus). To cross the Grand Canal, which functions as Venice's long main street, there are two main bridges, the Rialto and the Accademia.

Taxis are large motorboats; large deliveries are made by water, and smaller ones by hand truck. Garbage is removed from the Grand Canal, Venice's main street, by small boats with a metal-gridded scoop at the front. Lines for electricity and gas pipelines run underwater across the lagoon from the mainland. Police officers and firefighters use boats to do their jobs. It is even possible to reach the airport, named after the Venetian explorer Marco Polo, by taking a boat.

The Canale Grande, or Grand Canal, is Venice's main thoroughfare and curves through the city for 2 miles (almost 3 km).

Gondolas are traditional black Venetian boats. They are powered by a gondolier, who uses a long oar to push and steer the boat along. He stands at the back of the gondola and leans on his oar sticking out on the left of the boat.

The city came into being during the fifth and sixth centuries when people escaping from the tribes invading from the north came from the nearby mainland and took refuge in the islands of the lagoon. The refugees built on the flat islands by sinking thousands and thousands of wooden piles to make foundations for their houses. To go from one island to another, they built bridges. As the city and its buildings grew, these separate islands became the city of Venice. It is built on 117 small islands, and has 400 bridges crossing its 150 canals.

The best way to gain a first impression of Venice is to take a *vaporetto* down the Grand Canal. It is 2 miles (about 3 km) long and twists in an S-shape through the city. On the way it passes fine palaces built centuries ago. Their typical windows go up into a point, something like a Gothic arch. At the south end is the Piazza San Marco, Venice's main square. On three sides it has three-story stone buildings with arcades at ground level. Small orchestras play in three of the street-level cafés.

On the fourth side of the square is the Basilica San Marco, the richly decorated Byzantine basilica dedicated to St. Mark, Venice's patron saint. The symbol of the city is a winged lion which carries a sword in its right front paw. Next to the Basilica is the pink-and-white patterned Doge's Palace, built in the 14th century. From here the doge, or ruler, of Venice and the republic's government controlled the city's affairs.

Water, Water, Everywhere

Every year between 1173 and 1797 the Venetians held a ceremony where they rowed out into the lagoon. The doge, the ruler of Venice, dropped a gold ring into the sea, saying "We wed thee, sea, in token of our perpetual rule."

The idea of the ceremony was to show the Venetians' power over the sea, but they are often reminded of the sea and its power. Sometimes when the tide is high, large puddles of water form across the Piazza San Marco. When a very high tide is expected, usually in winter, sirens are sounded three to four hours before. On every *vaporetto* (waterbus) station, there are maps showing safe routes when the tide is exceptionally high and floods parts of the city.

High tides are made worse by the fact that the city is sinking. For many years engineers have discussed building a system of floodgates to protect Venice from the effect of high tides.

VENICE

SAN MICHELE

Ghetto

CANNAREGIO

Parking

GRAND CANAL

Station

SAN POLO

Rialto Bridge

Maritime Station

Arsenal

San Marco

SAN MARCO

Doge's Palace

SAN MICHELE

Accademia Bridge

San Giorgio Maggiore

Public Gardens

LA GIUDECCA

Church of Il Redentore

N

There was a network of spies to report on activities which were considered against the interests of the Venetian Republic. Enemies of the state were put in prison. The way through the palace to the prison goes over the Bridge of Sighs. The bridge is named because of the sighs made by prisoners as they crossed over. The other famous Venetian bridge is the Rialto, which crosses the Grand Canal and was a trading center during the Renaissance

Away from the broad Grand Canal many of the streets are more like a maze of narrow alleyways that spread out from central squares. The city is divided into districts called *sestrieri*. Every house in a *sestriere* is numbered, as well as being in a street. An address in the district of San Polo might be given as San Polo 1789, but to know how to get there, you have to know that that house is on Calle Sturion. In the San Marco district the house numbers go right up to 5562.

The main part of the Venetian islands is bisected by the Grand Canal. The historic center of government lay around San Marco, and the Arsenal, where Venice's impressive fleet was built, stood to the east.

Past and Present

"Now we've made Italy, let's make Italians"

Nineteenth-century Italian independence fighter Francesco Crispi

The land of Italy has been a meeting place of cultures for thousands of years. Its central position in the Mediterranean linked it with the trade routes of the ancient civilizations that developed in the region. Maritime trade with Phoenicia (near present-day Lebanon) and the states of ancient Greece brought profound cultural changes.

With the rise of Rome, however, the peninsula itself became the center of the ancient world, controlling the largest and most powerful empire the world had ever seen. It was to the capital of this empire that the first Christians came, so that with the fall of Rome in A.D. 476, the city became the center for the new religion. The spiritual and temporal power exerted by a succession of Italian popes in the following 1,000 years stretched over most of Europe. The artistic flowering of the Renaissance was a product of flourishing mercantile city-states, such as Florence and Venice. Thereafter, Italy's history was one of gradual decline and foreign domination. It was only with the independence movement of the mid-19th century that the many separate states of the Italian peninsula were unified.

The last century of Italian history has been among its most turbulent. First there was the rise of fascism and, after World War II, the threat of terrorism and corruption at the heart of the Italian state.

Many of the buildings in Rome's Forum were destroyed by fire in the third century A.D. Thereafter many of the same stones were used to build churches.

EARLY PEOPLES

The spread of human occupation in Italy began early in comparison to northern Europe. Since 2000 B.C. many different peoples have settled there. Around 1200 B.C. the Ligurians and the Italics came down from the north. The Ligurians were Bronze-Age settlers who moved down from what is now southern France and came to live in central Italy, near present-day Rome. The Italics came from near the Danube River in Central Europe.

MAGNA GRAECIA AND ETRURIA

People from the eastern end of the Mediterranean explored the coast of Italy from about 5000 B.C. The Phoenicians founded Carthage, in North Africa, and set up trading posts in Italy. By the eighth century B.C., the Greeks began to found colonies in Sicily and southern Italy. Altogether these colonies—including Syracuse, Agrigento, Crotone, and Taranto—were called Magna Graecia (Greater Greece).

Philosophers, scientists, and writers came to live in the Greek colonies, and cities were built with large temples and open-air theaters. At Agrigento in Sicily (*see* p. 28) and at Paestum near Naples, parts of the temples remain.

While the Greeks were settling southern Italy and Sicily, in central Italy the Etruscans were founding cities. The Etruscans are still something of a mystery. No one is sure where they came from originally. At first the Etruscans occupied the areas around the Arno and Tiber Rivers and the Apennines. Later they moved up into the Po Plain and down toward Rome. A federation of 12 city-states—including Volterra, Fiesole, Arezzo, Perugia, and Chiusi—made up the region of central Italy that we now know as Etruria.

These Etruscan terracotta horses come from the Ara della Regina temple in Tarquinia near Rome. They date to the third century B.C.

The Etruscans became rich by mining iron, copper, and silver and trading around the eastern Mediterranean area. Their cities were built on high ground and surrounded by defensive walls. They also built bridges, streets, and canals, and developed the use of the arch and barrel vault.

THE ROMAN REPUBLIC

The first Roman settlement was greatly influenced by its civilized Etruscan neighbors. At first it was ruled by kings. Both the Etruscans and the Romans coexisted peacefully until the defeat of the Etruscans at Veii and the incorporation of the town into Roman territory in 396 B.C. Over the next hundred years the Romans took over the former Etruscan territory.

The founding of Rome is officially dated to 753 B.C., from this time it was ruled by a line of seven kings. Early Rome was a regional center largely administered by several powerful families. The republic was set up in 509 B.C. so that no single family could take power. The republic made the people of Rome the ultimate authority, although in reality power was concentrated in the hands of a few families. Every year two consuls were elected; one looked after the army and the other was responsible for state administration.

There was also a senate. It was a kind of assembly that discussed and approved laws. The senators came from the most important aristocratic families in Rome. Roman citizens usually wore a toga, a loose robe made of one piece of cloth wrapped round the body. Consuls

ETRURIA c. 530 B.C.

Adria
Spina
Felsina • Ravenna
Siena
Populonia • Perusia
Clusium
ETRURIA • Volsinii
Vulci •
Tarquinia • Veii
Caere • Rome
Telesia
Campua • Neapolis
CAMPANIA
SARDINIA
Adriatic Sea
Tyrrhenian Sea
SICILY
N

The map shows the high point of Etruscan civilization in the sixth century B.C. The names of many of today's Italian cities, such as Perugia (Perusia), Naples (Neapolis), and Ravenna, had Etruscan names.

Rome's conquest of Greece and of the former Greek terrritories in the second and first centuries B.C. had a profound effect on the cultural life of the empire. The hitherto practical and rather coarse Roman republic was transformed into a center of learning. Greek ideas flourished in the success of Roman civilization.

wore a special white toga with a purple border to show their status. The ordinary people were called plebians and had no role in public affairs. Ten tribunes of the people represented them in government offices.

The Romans began to expand their territory, fighting and later forming alliances with the other tribes of Latium (the area around Rome). These were the Sabines, the Aequi, and the Volsci.

Other tribes came to challenge the Romans. In 390 B.C. the Gauls crossed the Alps and defeated the Roman army. Rome was almost destroyed and had to be rebuilt.

By 338 B.C. the Romans had conquered their former allies, including the Etruscans. The Samnites, the last of these Italian peoples, were defeated in 290 B.C.

In the eastern Mediterranean, the Greeks also began to worry that the Romans would become too powerful and want to take over Magna Graecia. In 280 B.C. King Pyrrus landed an army of 25,000 men in southern Italy. They defeated the Romans in two battles, but the Greek army lost 8,000 soldiers. There was a third battle, where more Greek soldiers were killed, and Pyrrus took his army back to Greece, leaving the Romans in control of the whole peninsula. A "Pyrrhic victory" still means a victory that is won at too high a cost.

The Carthaginians, who had their capital at Carthage in North Africa and colonies in Sardinia and western Sicily, were worried that the Romans would take over their Mediterranean trade. Between 264 and 146 B.C., the Romans defeated the Carthaginians in three wars, known as the Punic Wars.

Very Civilized!

Life as a wealthy Roman was very comfortable. The Romans lived in large villas. The main rooms of the house opened off a central atrium, or courtyard, with a pool in the center. The floors were decorated with beautiful mosaics of trees, plants, and scenes from legends or everyday life, and walls had bright frescoes. In winter there was central heating under the floors. In the dining room long couches were set around the table, so Romans could lie down while eating. The hard housework was done by slaves, who had been sold into slavery by poor families or captured in war.

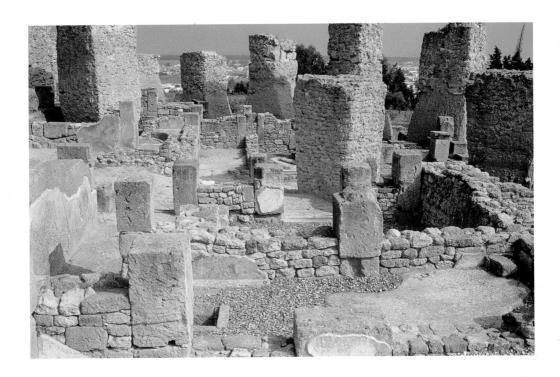

Gradually more territories were added to Rome's empire. Hispania (the Iberian Peninsula encompassing present-day Spain and Portugal) was ceded by the Carthaginians after the Second Punic War. By 146 B.C., Greece was a province of Rome. Other areas around the shores of the eastern Mediterranean were also under Roman control. By 49 B.C. the whole of Gallia (Gaul), including all of modern France, was part of the Roman empire, and Rome controlled the Mediterranean.

As the Roman territories became larger, rivalry developed among ambitious generals who wanted to take control. With their armies, generals like Sulla, Pompey, and Julius Caesar made power bases in the provinces from which they threatened the central government in Rome. After a civil war in which he defeated his fellow consul, Pompey, Julius Caesar became the dictator of Rome. Rome was no longer a republic. Although he was a clever ruler, Caesar's increasing arrogance annoyed the Romans. In 44 B.C. he was assassinated at the Senate by those who wanted to restore the republic.

Part of the remains of Carthage, now in Tunisia, once the center of a great trading empire that rivaled the Romans in the Mediterranean.

THE EXPANSION OF THE ROMAN EMPIRE

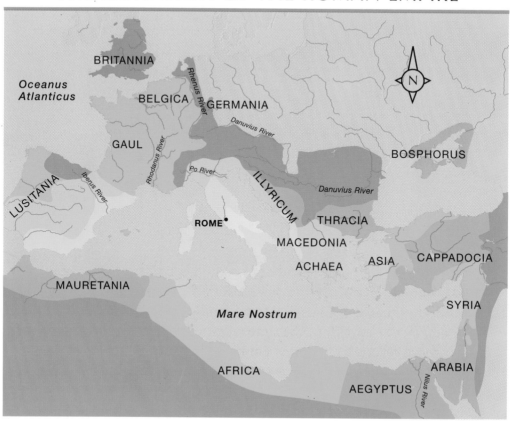

By 300 B.C.
By 270 B.C.
By 200 B.C.
By 133 B.C.
By 27 B.C.
By A.D. 117
Unconquered lands

The greatest expansion of Roman power started in the first century B.C.

THE FIRST EMPEROR

The ruler who followed Julius Caesar became Rome's first emperor. He was Caesar's great-nephew, Octavian, who took control after Caesar's death. He reorganized the administration of Rome. In 27 B.C. he took the title of Augustus (sacred). During his long reign of more than 40 years, Augustus Caesar brought stability to the Roman empire.

When Augustus Caesar died in A.D. 14, his son Tiberius became emperor. Tiberius was followed by Augustus' grandson, Caligula, in A.D. 37. Caligula ruled for only four years, until he was assassinated. He did many strange and cruel things during his reign. He had his wife, Drusilla, put to death, and had his horse appointed as a consul.

An International Language

The language of the Romans was called Latin. It takes its name from Latium, the area around the city of Rome. Latin was used across the Roman empire. Later the Catholic church also used Latin as its official language. In the Middle Ages between A.D. 476 and 1453, it was an international language used for official documents and by university students. It is still used in the naming of species.

You may think you do not know any Latin, but we use Latin words in English all the time. When you're talking about the time, you probably say A.M. or P.M. to show if you are talking about the morning or the afternoon. You are using Latin. The letters A.M. stand for *ante meridiem*, before midday, and P.M. for *post meridiem*, after midday. Now check out A.D. and etc. in a dictionary.

The next emperor was Claudius, Caligula's uncle. Claudius was an efficient ruler who added Britannia (Britain) to the empire in A.D. 42. After Claudius died in A.D. 54, his adopted son Nero became emperor.

In the years of Nero's reign as emperor, Rome was filled with stories of his cruelty. A large part of the city was damaged by fire in A.D. 64, and Nero blamed the Christians, followers of a new religion. He had them persecuted and tortured. He had both of his wives murdered. Finally the Roman Senate condemned Nero to death, but he committed suicide.

After Nero's death there was confusion as to who should rule Rome. For the second half of the first century, a number of emperors brought stability and a better life for the people of Rome. In A.D. 69 a general called Vespasian took control, and became an efficient emperor. Under Emperor Trajan's reign from 98 to 117, the Roman empire reached

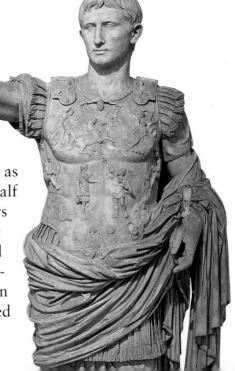

Augustus Caesar, who ruled for 45 years, boasted that he found Rome a city of brick and left it a city of marble.

Diocletian made huge administrative changes in the empire and in the Roman army. In A.D. 303 one of his edicts began a decade of persecution against the Christians.

This Roman sarcophagus (stone coffin) of Livia Primitiva from the early third century has the Christian symbols of the fish, good shepherd, and anchor inscribed on it.

its greatest extent. Hadrian, who followed Trajan, reorganized Roman laws and had defensive forts built along the imperial borders.

In order to make administering such a vast empire easier, Emperor Diocletian (A.D. 245–313) divided it into eastern and western parts. The western capital was still in Rome, while the eastern capital was at Byzantium (present-day Istanbul, Turkey). Diocletian chose to rule from Byzantium.

A NEW RELIGION

Jesus Christ lived and died in a Roman province: Palestine. After his death the new religion of Christianity became popular among people in the Roman empire, but it was forbidden. Christians could be persecuted, punished, or even executed for their religion, so they worshiped secretly. Things changed when Constantine the Great became emperor.

There was trouble in the Roman empire because the eastern and western parts threatened to break apart.

Before a battle in A.D. 313, Constantine's army looked very weak compared to the enemy forces. Legend has it that Constantine saw a cross glowing in the midday sky, with some words written in Greek, meaning "In this sign, conquer." He made a promise that, if he won the battle, he would allow Christians to worship freely. Just before his death in A.D. 337, Constantine was baptized a Christian. Christianity later became the official religion of the Roman empire.

In the second half of the fifth century the Barbarian tribes formed distinct political units. Their cohesion threatened Rome and the city finally fell in A.D. 476.

After Constantine died, there were more and more invasions from tribes living on the northern borders of the empire. Many of them were being attacked themselves, as the Huns, lead by Attila, pushed across from central Asia. The Anglo-Saxons invaded the province of Britannia. The Burgundians occupied the area between the Rhine and the Rhone Rivers, while the Franks gradually took over western Gallia.

By A.D. 410 a Visigoth army, lead by Alaric, captured Rome. Later they left the Italian peninsula and settled in the region of southern France and Spain. The end of the Roman empire came in A.D. 476, when Odoacer, a Barbarian leader, deposed the emperor Romulus Augustulus from the throne. It was the end of the Roman empire in the west, although the Romans continued to rule the eastern part of the empire from Byzantium.

BARBARIAN INVASIONS IN THE FIFTH CENTURY

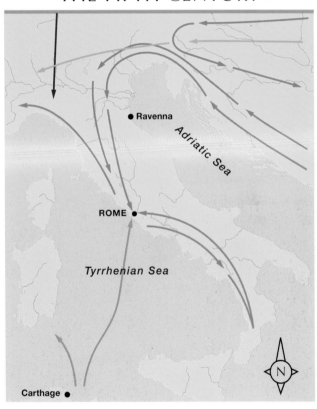

Ravenna

Adriatic Sea

ROME

Tyrrhenian Sea

Carthage

N

→ Huns
→ Ostrogoths
→ Visigoths
→ Vandals
→ Lombards

CHARLEMAGNE

After the fall of the Roman empire, different people struggled for control of the Italian peninsula. The only areas with some order were on the east coast from Ravenna down to Ancona, Puglia, and Calabria, which remained under the control of the eastern emperor at Byzantium. Rome was governed by the pope.

Around A.D. 560 a Germanic tribe called the Lombards invaded Italy. There were not many of them, but they took advantage of the confusion to push down the peninsula, destroying towns as they went.

The Lombards converted to Christianity, made laws, and began to rebuild towns and cities and encourage trade and agriculture. The daughters of the Lombard

CHARLEMAGNE'S EMPIRE IN 814

*This map shows
the extent of
Charlemagne's empire
at his death in 814.
Although illiterate
himself, Charlemagne
was responsible for
great advances in
the promotion of
learning and culture
within his realm.*

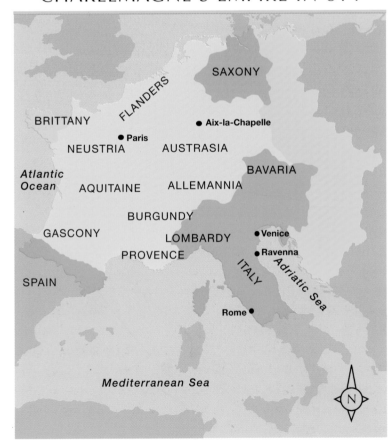

Frankish
kingdom 768

Conquests of
Charlemagne
768–814

Dependent terri-
tories 814

Unaligned
territories

king married the sons of the Frankish king, but later when the Lombards tried to settle the power struggles between two Frankish leaders, war broke out between the Lombards and the Franks.

The Frankish leader, Charlemagne, conquered Lombard areas in Italy. In Rome, on Christmas Day in A.D. 800, the pope crowned Charlemagne Holy Roman emperor. His name means Charles the Great. Italy was divided into three parts: Lombardy, the Papal States, and the south, which was still under Byzantine control. The Lombards and the Franks encouraged loyalty from their followers by using the feudal system. Land was given to noblemen by the king. In return he expected the noblemen to take an oath to be loyal to him and to pay him money or goods every year. The noblemen had to bring soldiers to fight for the king in times of war. In turn the nobleman gave parts of his land to others, who promised to be loyal to him.

The troops of Charlemagne lay siege to the city of Rome, in an illustration from a medieval manuscript, now in the National Library in Turin.

Noblemen had the power of life or death over the people who lived in the areas they controlled. The serfs who worked the land had to do work for their lord. They had no protection or rights if the lord was unjust in the way he treated them and they were not permitted to read or write, or make money. They were not allowed to move away to try and make a living somewhere else, because they were "tied" to a lord.

THE MARITIME REPUBLICS

Some coastal cities had protected themselves against the invasions after the fall of the Roman empire. They constructed defensive walls, forts, and good harbors, and built up powerful fleets. By trading goods around the Mediterranean, they brought wealth to Italy.

Beginning in the ninth century these coastal cities became the maritime republics. The most important were Venice, Pisa, and Genoa, and farther south, Amalfi. They fought off and defeated pirates from the North African coast, and often set up trading bases a long way from their home cities.

Trade brought not only wealth but also knowledge. Many technical and commercial developments came from the Muslim world, including the use of modern numbers, which we incorrectly call "Arabic" but were in fact derived from an Indian script.

For the maritime republics it was not the conquest of large areas of territory that was important, but the control of trading routes and strategic ports throughout the Mediterranean area.

THE MARITIME REPUBLICS

FRANCE

HOLY ROMAN EMPIRE

HUNGARY

Genoa

Venice

Pisa • Florence

Black Sea

Rome

Constantinople

Naples • Bari

Amalfi Taranto

OTTOMAN EMPIRE

Palermo

Mediterranean Sea

☐ Ottoman Empire
☐ Holy Roman Empire
☐ Territory of Amalfi
☐ Venetian territory
☐ Pisan territory
☐ Genoan territory
☰ Pisan/Genoan territory
△ Venetian bases
△ Genoan bases
△ Pisan bases

N

The Venetian Empire

The Most Serene Republic of Venice, or "La Serenissima," was run by a leader called the doge, with the help of two advisory councils. People who were thought to be enemies of the Republic were put in prison.

Initially the city owed its allegiance to the Byzantine empire based at Constantinople, and Byzantium granted the city extensive trading rights in the eastern Mediterranean. It was with the trade generated by the Crusades, however, that the city truly came into its own. With the sack of Constantinople in 1204 came effective control of the eastern Mediterranean, further secured by the defeat of its main rival, Genoa, in the War of Chioggia (1379–1380).

Venetians were clever business people who were happy to trade with all nations, whatever their religion or politics. At the height of the republic's success, Venetian territories included parts of northern Italy, the Adriatic coast around Venice and farther east, parts of mainland Greece, and many of the Aegean islands near Greece, including Crete and Cyprus. The Venetians became

famous as plunderers and their art and architecture showed a strong influence from the Middle East.

A Venetian trader, Marco Polo, went as far as China to find out about trade goods like silk and spices. He was given a position at the Chinese emperor's court and later brought back tales of China in addition to trade goods.

Venetian commerce declined when Europeans landed in the Americas in the late 15th century. The rise of the Ottoman empire led to the loss of territories in the Mediterranean. After 1600 trade began to be centered on Europe's Atlantic ports, not on the Mediterranean. In 1797 Napoleon finally brought the Venetian empire to an end. In 1815 the city passed to the Austrian Hapsburg empire until unification with the rest of Italy.

THE POPE AND THE EMPEROR

Muslim pirates invaded Italy from Africa and Spain and in 846 looted Rome, forcing the pope Leo IV to build a defensive wall around the Vatican, which can still be seen today. Muslims settled in Sicily where they remained for 200 years.

From the tenth century on Rome was the center of the Christian world. The pope organized the Catholic church from his territories in central Italy. The pope had crowned the first Holy Roman emperor—a Germanic emperor ruling much of what is now central mainland Europe. However, there were constant struggles between the church and the Holy Roman emperor. They became rivals as the church extended its lands and its influence in European politics. The struggles between the empire and the papacy continued for centuries.

During the 11th century the people living in cities in the north and center of Italy wanted to live freely. They declared themselves free from the rule of the Holy Roman emperor and the pope, deciding to elect their own judges, make their own laws, have their own currency, and create alliances and make war without having to consult any other cities.

Once they had established these rights, the people of a *comune* (city-state) were ready to fight to defend

The Visconti of Milan

The Visconti family rose to prominence in the 11th century, transforming their family title of viscount into their surname. Pope Urban IV appointed Ottone Visconti archbishop of Milan in 1262, and the head of the Visconti family then acquired the titles of vicar and *signore* (lord) of Milan. During the 13th and 14th centuries the family made marriage alliances with French and German princes. In the 1350s the influence of the Visconti stretched as far as the cities of Genoa and Bologna. During this period the family was also involved in wars with the popes and with the city-state of Florence. By the beginning of the 15th century the Visconti ruled most of northern Italy with the exception of Venice and Florence—Pisa, Siena, Bologna, and Perugia all lay under Visconti control. This was also a period of great artistic patronage: the poet Petrarch was a member of the Visconti court. In 1447 the Venetian army marched on Milan and Filippo Maria Visconti appealed to his son-in-law, the mercenary Francesco Sforza, for help. The city was defended and on Filippo Maria's death the Visconti state passed to Sforza.

them. Sometimes there were difficulties when the citizens of the *comune* could not agree among themselves and split into groups, or when nearby towns supported different sides. Two of the best known political parties were the Guelfs (supporters of the pope) and the Ghibellines (supporters of the emperor). Fighting between the city-states allowed tyrannical rulers to take power. A powerful family could rule a city-state for years. The Visconti family ruled Milan (*see* opposite), the Della Scala in Verona, the Gonzagas in Mantua, and the Medici in Florence.

Some cities paid mercenaries to protect them from the bandits who also roamed the land. These groups of paid soldiers were led by a *condottiere*, who negotiated the contract for protection.

In the south of Italy the situation was different. Sicily had been invaded and settled by Muslims in the ninth and tenth centuries. The Normans had pushed the Saracens out in the 11th and 12th centuries and established the Kingdom of the Two Sicilies. Cities like Naples and other territories in southern Italy were added by conquest. Emperor Frederick II inherited Sicily in 1198, and wanted to control all of Italy.

When he died, the pope gave his kingdom to the brother of the king of France. In 1282 a revolt broke out and a 30-year war—the War of the Sicilian Vespers—started. The Sicilians turned to the Spanish for help. The Spanish beat the French and took over Sicily.

The crest of the six Medici balls is to be found on many buildings in Pisa and Siena, wealthy cities that became vassals of the Florentine family firm.

THE RENAISSANCE

By the end of the 14th century many city-states—including Milan, Bologna, Florence, Mantua, and Verona—had established their independence. Like the maritime republics, the city-states became important trade centers.

With money from trade, wealthy families were able to build fine houses and public buildings. The Gothic-style cathedral in Milan was started in 1396. In Florence sculptors and artists worked on decorating the Palazzo Vecchio for the ruling Medici family (*see* below).

Inspired by the art and philosophy of the Romans and the Greeks, many artists explored new ideas. Beginning in Italy and then spreading to other countries, this revival in learning was called the *Rinascimento*, meaning "rebirth." We use the French word Renaissance for it. It lasted through the 15th and 16th centuries.

There were also many discoveries in science and advances in technology. The dukes of Florence, for example, set up a society of astronomers and other scientists.

The lavish decoration of the Sala dei Gigli in the Palazzo Vecchio in Florence shows the extent of patronage (support of artists) by Italy's ruling families. The fresco here is by Domenico Ghirlandaio and was painted in around 1482.

In the Bank

As Italian city-states developed their trade, they organized systems for making payments in different countries and continents. This meant that merchants did not have to travel around with large, heavy bags of gold or silver coins, and risk being robbed on their journey. Traders used a system of bills of exchange, which could be changed for a certain amount of money, like traveler's checks (*see* right).

Many terms in modern banking have an Italian origin, even the word "bank." It comes from the *banca*, the table or bench that was used as a counter in a trading office. Italian traders from Genoa, Florence, Venice, and Siena, also developed a sophisticated bookkeeping system for their accounts.

ITALIAN EXPLORERS

Explorers from Italian cities went to many corners of the world. Christopher Columbus, a navigator from Genoa, was sure that by crossing the Atlantic and continuing west he could reach India. Venetian traders had traveled overland to India to bring back spices, perfumes, scented wood, and precious stones. In the 15th century, war between the Turks and the Venetians made this journey impossible.

Columbus explained his idea to people in Genoa and Naples, even to the pope, but they were not interested. Finally King Ferdinand and Queen Isabella of Spain sponsored him. With three small ships, the *Niña*, the *Pinta*, and the *Santa María*, he set off from southern Spain on August 3, 1492.

After a long and exhausting voyage, the ships made landfall in a new land on October 12. Columbus called the people he came across "Indians," because he thought that he was in India. Only after more voyages did Columbus realize that he had reached a "new world." Later, another Italian, Amerigo Vespucci (1454–1512), explored the coast of South America. The name for the Americas comes from a Latin version of his first name, Americus. Farther north, the Venetian Giovanni Caboto (1450–1499), known as John Cabot, explored along the coast of present-day Canada for the king of England, Henry VII.

Columbus' voyage to America was a product of the advances in seamanship made by the trading city-states of Genoa, Pisa, and Venice during the 14th and 15th centuries.

A BATTLEGROUND

In the 16th century Italy was a collection of city-states and kingdoms which were often controlled by foreign powers. In 1530 the Spanish king, who was also the Holy Roman emperor, controlled many areas of Italy. Milan and parts of Tuscany, in addition to Naples, Sicily, and Sardinia, were under his control. Venice, Genoa, Mantua, Savoy, and the Papal States were still independent. The time would come, however, when Italy's rich trading routes would become irresistible to the central European powers and previously independent areas would be merged together.

THE ITALIAN STATES IN 1454

HOLY ROMAN EMPIRE

ROME

KINGDOM OF NAPLES

SARDINIA

Tyrrhenian Sea

SICILY

N

	Papal States
	Venice
	Naples
	Milan
	Genoa
	Savoy
	Siena
	Mantua
	Ferrara
	Montferrat
	Lucca
	Saluzzo
	Modena
	Piombino
	Florence
———	extent of Holy Roman empire

The many competing states on the Italian peninsula in the 15th century made the region vulnerable to attack from foreign powers.

During the 17th century the peninsula of Italy became a battleground for different European powers who wanted to conquer the country. Economic power passed away from the Italian city-states and toward the European powers establishing overseas colonies. In the Thirty Years' War (1618–1648) and the War of the Spanish Succession (1701–1714) areas of Italy passed from one power to another. The Austrians, French, and Spanish sent their armies to fight each other. Lombardy, Mantua, Naples, and Sardinia fell under Austrian control, while Piedmont passed to the Duke of Savoy. In the mid-1730s the last of the Medici died and Tuscany

The Grand Tour

A taste for all things classical had been gathering steam in Europe throughout the early 18th century. However, it was the discovery of the buried town of Pompeii outside Naples in 1748 that really fired the enthusiasm of educated Europeans for relics of the Roman empire. During the mid-18th century Italy began to be popular as a destination for the younger members of the European aristocracy. A young person's education was felt to be incomplete until they had savored the classical delights of Greece and Rome, the elegant ruins inspired the Romantic imagination. Wealthier visitors were able to buy up large amounts of statuary, frescoes, and even entire buildings. Rome became the main destination for a tour of the classical sites, the Grand Tour.

Napoleon's coronation as king of Italy turned into a stand-off with Pope Pius VII. Insulted at being summoned to Paris, the pope arrived days late. So annoyed was Bonaparte that when it came to the coronation he snatched the crown from Pius and crowned himself.

passed to the French house of Lorraine. In the latter half of the 18th century much of northern Italy was controlled by Austria while the south lay largely under Bourbon control.

It was only with the rise of the French leader Napoleon Bonaparte toward the end of the 18th century that nationalism began in earnest. French armies invaded northern Italy in 1796 and set up a series of republics. The Cisalpine Republic had its capital at Milan and the Ligurian Republic at Genoa. There was also a Roman Republic in Rome and a Parthenopean Republic, centered on Naples. Later Napoleon made these areas into an Italian kingdom and made himself king in 1806. This state of affairs lasted until 1815, when Bonaparte was defeated at the Battle of Waterloo and his empire was dismantled.

Italy was divided up again. The Austrians took Lombardy and Venice. Piedmont-Sardinia in the northwest became an independent kingdom. The Spanish controlled the Kingdom of the Two Sicilies (Sicily and the area of the Italian peninsula south of the Papal States), and the pope ruled in the Papal States.

UNITED ITALY

Although Italy had not been united since the time of the Romans, Italians were influenced by the ideas of liberty from the French Revolution and wanted to unite their country. Three men were central in the struggle to free Italy and make it a nation.

Giuseppe Mazzini (1805–1872) wrote articles about political freedom and joined one of the secret societies that promoted a united Italy. He was put in prison, but on his release was even more determined to help his country. In 1831 he set up the Young Italy movement. After a failed revolt Mazzini was sent into exile in London, England.

While Mazzini was trying to inspire people to fight for a united Italy, Count Camillo Cavour (1810–1861) founded a newspaper called *Il Risorgimento* ("the Resurrection") in Piedmont. The name of his newspaper was later taken for the movement to unify Italy. There were many revolutions across Europe in 1848, and Cavour joined people from Lombardy and Venice who were fighting the Austrian empire. They failed, but Vittorio Emanuele II, who was king of Piedmont-Sardinia, made Cavour chief minister. With the help of the French, in 1859 the Piedmontese army defeated the Austrians at the battles of Magenta and Solferino.

Garibaldi, the leader of the Italian nationalist movement, was actually born in Nice, now in France, and spent 12 years in Uruguay before returning to Italy to fight in the republican army.

The third principal figure in the Risorgimento was Giuseppe Garibaldi (1807–1882). Because of his association with Mazzini, he had to leave Italy and spent many years in the United States and in South America. In 1854 he came back and fought with the king of Piedmont-Sardinia's army against the Austrians.

As Vittorio Emmanuele's army moved toward the south, Garibaldi went to Sicily in 1860. He landed with a thousand volunteers, who took the island. The army

THE FIGHT FOR INDEPENDENCE

While Garibaldi traveled to Sicily to launch an attack from the south, Cavour and Vittorio Emmanuele marched Piedmontese troops down the peninsula. Only after France had been defeated by the Prussians, and the French had been ousted from Rome, did the city become the Italian capital in 1871.

Territory ceded to other states

Italy 1861

Battles

Route of Garibaldi's Thousand 1860

Route of Vittorio Emmanuele II 1860

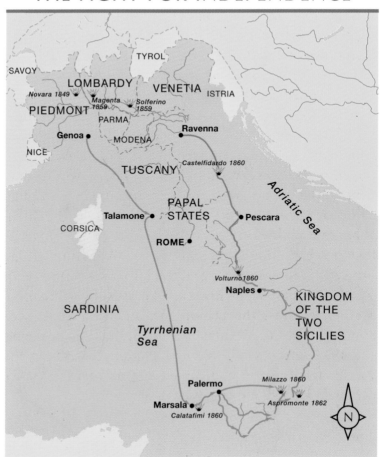

then marched north and captured Naples. The two armies met at Teano on October 26. Vittorio Emmanuele was proclaimed king of Italy, and Turin became the capital. By 1861 almost all of Italy was united. Five years later the Austrians gave up Venice, and finally in 1870 the pope allowed the Papal States to become part of Italy. Italy was a country again, with its capital in Rome.

MAKING A NATION

Italy was united, but people had very different ideas about what kind of country they wanted. At first many politicians concentrated more on the problems of making Italy a nation. Among others things they had to organize the administrative and legal system, the mail service, and public schools. The national road and railroad networks were expanded. To finance all of this, high taxes had to be imposed on the people.

Garibaldi was keen to see a lot of social reforms. In 1876 a more left-wing government introduced five years of free but compulsory elementary-school education. The voting system was reformed, so that anyone who had studied at elementary school could vote. At the same time industry was developing in Italy. Workers organized themselves into groups to demand better rights.

Abroad, Italy began to expand its trade with Africa. It became more ambitious and tried to take over territory in Ethiopia (then known as Abyssinia). The Ethiopians fought back, and the Italians were left with the small territory of Eritrea. The Somalis asked Italy for help against the Ethiopians, and Italy took over Somalia, too. In 1911 and 1912 the Italians invaded and occupied Libya. None of these conquests brought the wealth the Italians had hoped for, as the areas they occupied were mainly poor or desert lands.

The International Situation

The isolation of the new Italian state during the 1870s was made more severe by the French occupation of Tunisia in 1881. Dissatisfaction with France led the Italians to form an alliance with Germany and the Austro-Hungarian empire in 1882. The alliance secured Italian interests in the Mediterranean against French expansion but Italian imperialist ambitions now turned to North Africa. These can be seen as part of the European powers' "Scramble for Africa," the eagerness of the industrialized powers to establish colonies providing raw materials to feed the factories that supported their economies. Despite Italian raids into east Africa in 1889, a full-scale Italo-French conflict was averted by an agreement in 1902 that effectively gave each country a separate sphere of influence. This resulted in the Italian invasion of Libya in 1911 and the Italo-Turkish War of 1911–1912. Eventually, however, the earlier alliance with Germany and Austria was to bring about a far greater penalty from the Italian nation.

A WORLD WAR

Pope Pius IX initially refused to recognize the Kingdom of Italy and was stripped of his governmental powers and of the Quirinale Palace. It was only with the accession of the Fascist Party to power that the papacy regained its self-government.

In 1882, Italy had became part of the Triple Alliance with two important powers of central and northern Europe: Germany and Austria. The other major European powers–Russia, France, Britain—formed another alliance.

Within the German and Austrian empires, there were people of other ethnic origins who wanted to be independent. On June 28, 1914, a Serb nationalist named Gavrilo Princip assassinated Archduke Franz Ferdinand, who was the heir to the Austrian empire. Austria held the Serbian government responsible and declared war.

The war might not have lasted long if the Russians had not become involved. Austria's ally, Germany, also declared war on Serbia, Russia, and its ally, France. Britain came to support France. World War I had begun.

Italy stayed neutral until 1915, when it declared war on Austria and Germany. The Italians hoped to win back territories in Austria with large Italian populations that they thought should join Italy.

The Italians fought along the Alps, sheltering from the intense cold in trenches. The hardest fighting took place in June 1918, but in October the Italian soldiers beat the Germans at the battle of Vittorio Veneto.

Italian troops of the 35th infantry division in 1916.

MUSSOLINI

After World War I, Europe went through difficult times. In Russia there was a revolution and a communist government took over. Italy had to face serious financial problems, and jobs became hard to find. Many ordinary people thought life would be better if they had a socialist or communist system. The Popular Party and the socialists were the two main parties in the 1919 elections, but neither had a majority in parliament.

Another political movement developed: fascism. The leader was Benito Mussolini (1883–1945), who was an ex-socialist. Many of the fascists were ex-soldiers who could not get used to peace again and opposed the socialists. In 1922 the fascists marched on Rome, and King Vittorio Emmanuele III asked Mussolini to head the government.

Mussolini quickly became a dictator and banned legal opposition in parliament. Special squads threatened people who opposed Mussolini. The Italian parliament had almost no power. In 1936 Mussolini invaded Ethiopia once again to find a source of the raw materials that Italy lacked and to find markets for its goods.

At the same time, other dictators were taking control in Germany and in Spain. In 1938, Germany occupied its neighbor Austria and parts of Czechoslovakia. In 1939, Germany attacked Poland. France and Britain

Benito Mussolini was born at Predappio near Rimini and worked as a journalist, founding his own newspaper, Il Popolo d'Italia (The Italian People), before forming the Italian Fascist Party in 1921.

The Fascist Party took its name from the *fasces,* a bundle of elm or birch rods that symbolized official authority in ancient Rome. The fascists adopted it as their emblem in 1919.

declared war on Germany. Italy was Germany's ally and declared war on Greece. World War II had started.

After the Japanese bombed the U.S. naval base at Pearl Harbor, the United States entered the war on the side of the Allies. Italian and German armies in Africa were defeated by British and American soldiers, who moved on to Sicily. In Italy, power was given back to the king, and Mussolini was arrested. The Italians joined the side of the Allies. By the end of 1943, the south of Italy was under the control of British and American soldiers, while the north was occupied by the Germans. Some Italians became partisans, part of a secret army that hid in woods and mountains and fought against the Germans. Mussolini tried to escape to Switzerland, but he was caught and shot. The war in Europe ended in May 1945.

Italian partisans near the Alps in northern Italy bearing the Italian flag in February 1945.

A NEW REPUBLIC

After World War II Italy had to give up its African colonies. Part of Piedmont was given to France, and Istria to the east became part of Yugoslavia. In 1946 the Italians voted in a referendum to become a republic.

The first government after the war was dominated by the Christian Democrat Party led by Alcide De Gasperi (1881–1954), who won more than half the vote, but it also included members of the Socialist and Communist Parties in a coalition government. In 1947 De Gasperi formed a government that excluded socialists and communists.

During World War II bombing and fighting had destroyed towns, railroads, bridges, factories, and ports. Aid from the United States helped with machinery and raw materials for rebuilding the country.

Italian people worked hard to put the postwar years behind them and the standard of living improved. The Italian government set up a special fund—the *Cassa del Mezzogiorno* (the State Fund for the South)—to help develop the south of Italy. In 1957 Italy joined the European Economic Community with West Germany, France, Belgium, Luxembourg, and the Netherlands. By the 1960s, industry in the north of the country began to boom, particularly the automobile industry, and many people migrated from the poorer agricultural regions of the south to the booming cities of the north, such as Milan and Turin.

Former prime minister Aldo Moro is held hostage in 1976 by the Red Brigades. His body was later found in a car in the center of Rome equidistant from the headquarters of the two main political parties.

The Christian Democrat Party held power for nearly 50 years after World War II. However, the Communist Party formed an important opposition, with millions of registered members. During the late 1960s there were many student protests in Italy and in 1969 came the *Autumno Caldo* (the Hot Autumn), a period of strikes and unrest that continued into 1971.

The 1970s and the 1980s were marked by the rise of terrorism in Italy. Right-wing and left-wing groups were active. Neo-fascist groups planted bombs. In 1980, 84 people were killed in an explosion at the Bologna railroad station. Some extreme left-wing activists formed the Red Brigades (*Brigate Rosse*) and other groups. They wanted to break up the monopoly of the right-wing Christian Democrats on political power in Italy and improve social conditions. Business people, judges, university professors, a NATO general, and even an ex-prime minister, Aldo Moro (*see* above), were kidnapped or assassinated by the Red Brigades as a means of protesting against political inaction.

The years between 1973 and 1980 in Italy, the years of terrorism, were known as the *Anni di Piombo* or "Years of Lead."

The *Partito Demo-cratico della Sinistra* (PDS) took on many of the symbols of the old Italian Communist Party, including that of the oak tree.

In 1983, declining support for the Christian Democrats led them to enter into a coalition with the socialists and the country had its first socialist prime minister, Bettino Craxi (1934–1999). In the early 1990s, after the fall of communism in the Soviet Union and Eastern Europe, the Italian Communist Party split into two parts, the larger part (later the PDS, *see* left) abandoning many of the central policies of communism, with the smaller faction (*Rifondazione Communista*, Refounded Communists) sticking to its earlier principles.

THE MAFIA

The mafia has a long history in Italy. First emerging in Sicily in the medieval period, it began as a secret society attempting to throw off the yoke of the island's foreign rulers. The mafia took its name from the small private armies, or *mafie,* used by absentee landlords to protect their possessions. So harsh were the landowners that the mafia gained substantial support from the local people. The mafia's code of behavior was based on *omertà,* the principle of never helping the authorities in the detection of crimes, nor to give evidence against others. Revenge could only be taken by the victim of the crime.

By the early 20th century, "families" or groups of *mafiosi* controlled much of the economy of southern Italy. Mussolini's fascists nearly crushed the mafia by imprisoning many of its leaders. At the end of World War II, however, American occupation authorities released many of the *mafiosi* and the mafia began to take hold of emerging Italian industry in the south. During the later 20th century, huge sums from public works were siphoned off into mafia accounts, and cities such as Naples and Palermo were effectively controlled by *mafiosi.* It had long been accepted that the influence of the mafia spread to the highest level of Italian politics. In the early 1990s unraveling corruption scandals and confessions from captured mafia bosses linked the mafia with the former prime minister Giulio Andreotti, who had been virtually a permanent fixture in Italian politics since the war. In 1992, within two months, two judges, Giovanni Falcone and Paolo Borsellino, were murdered. Giovanni Falconi's car was blown up on a superhighway, killing the judge, his wife, the driver, and three police officers.

Since the 1980s the mafia has monopolized the drug trade in Italy. It still controls large areas of the south and has recently moved into the former communist economies of Eastern Europe.

The *Lega Nord*

The *Lega Nord,* or Northern League, first achieved electoral success in 1992, gaining 7 percent of the vote with their anti-corruption platform. The party was formed to oppose what it saw as the subsidizing of the poor south by the richer north. The League's leader Umberto Bossi has called for the establishment of a separate state called Padania in northern Italy, consisting of Veneto, Liguria Piedmont, Lombardy, Emilia-Romagna, and the small Alpine regions. He has advised northern Italians to withhold taxes from what he sees as the corrupt bureaucracy of Rome and the League has minted its own coin. Despite support for the League —in 1996 it gained 9 percent of the vote —most Italians strongly oppose division of their country. Bossi's portrayal of the south as corrupt was undermined by the *Tangentopoli* scandals unearthed in Milan, the League's hometown (*see* below).

TANGENTOPOLI AND ITS AFTERMATH

The major event of the last decade has been the unfolding of the *Tangentopoli* scandals. The name for a bribe is a *tangente*, and Italians called Milan, the center of the initial scandal, *Tangentopoli.* In 1992 a judge from Milan, Antonio di Pietro, started an investigation into corruption among politicians and business people who had accepted bribes in exchange for public works' contracts worth millions of dollars. This investigation was called Operation *Mani Pulite* ("Clean Hands").

The corruption reached to the heart of the Italian political establishment and members of almost all parties connected with government were implicated. In the national elections of 1994, support for the main political parties, particularly the Christian Democrats and the socialists, collapsed. As a result, the right-wing alliance known as the *Polo della Libertà* (Freedom Alliance) came to power. It was composed of the neofascist *Alleanza Nazionale* (National Alliance), the *Lega Nord* (Northern League, *see* box), and *Forza Italia* (Go Italy). The latter was led by the media tycoon Silvio Berlusconi (born 1936). The coalition collapsed after a matter of months. In the 1996 election a center-left coalition

Two years after becoming prime minister, Silvio Berlusconi himself came under investigation for corruption. A large number of charges were dismissed because of the lengthy process they took to pass through Italy's courts.

known as the Olive Tree Alliance won a majority led by the former professor, Romano Prodi (born 1940). Later governments have been concerned to balance Italy's economy and to pass the tough economic tests necessary for Italy to join the new euro currency.

POLITICAL ORGANIZATION

Italy is a democratic republic. The head of government is the prime minister, who is referred to in Italy as the President of the Council of Ministers. The prime minister chooses the government ministers and directs government policy. The chief of state is the president, whose role is largely ceremonial, although the position can involve important constitutional duties. This was particularly evident in the aftermath of the *Mani Pulite* investigation in 1994, when most of the Italian political establishment had been discredited and again after the fall of Berlusconi's government in the following year. After the fall of Berlusconi's government, Oscar Scalfaro appointed a caretaker team of adminstrators to run the country. It was clearly important that the president should be seen to be above party political bias in such a situation.

Italy's parliament is split into two chambers. Of the 315 seats in the Senate, 232 are directly elected and 83 are elected by regional proportional representation. There are also a number of senators for life, who include

THE ITALIAN PARLIAMENT IN 2000

President: Carlo Azeglio Ciampi

Senate
315 members • Last election 1996 • Elections held every five years

Olive Tree (Left-wing alliance)	50%
Freedom Alliance (Right-wing alliance)	37%
Lega Nord (Northern League)	9%
RC (Refounded Communists)	3%
others	1%

Chamber of Deputies
630 members • Last election 1996 • Elections held every five years

Olive Tree (Left-wing alliance)	45%
Freedom Alliance (Right-wing alliance)	39%
Lega Nord (Northern League)	9%
RC (Refounded Communists)	6%
others	1%

- G. Leone (1968)
- M. Rumor (1968–1970)
- E. Colombo (1970–1972)
- G. Andreotti (1972–1974)
- A. Moro (1974–1976)
- G. Andreotti (1976–1978)
- F. Cossiga (1979–1980)
- A. Forlani (1980–1981)
- G. Spadolini (1981–1982)
- A. Fanfani (1982–1983)
- B. Craxi (1983–1987)
- A. Fanfani (1987)
- G. Goria (1987–1988)
- C. De Mita (1988–1989)
- G. Andreotti (1989–1992)
- G. Amato (1992–1994)
- S. Berlusconi (1994)
- L. Dini (1994–1996)
- R. Prodi (1996–1998)
- M. D'Alema (1998–)

former presidents and leading figures from the establishment—these currently include the heads of the Fiat and Benetton companies. Senators are elected for five-year terms. Of the 630 seats in the Chamber of Deputies, 475 are directly elected and 155 are elected by proportional representation. Again, members serve five-year terms. The difference between the system of direct election and proportional representation is that with the former the candidate with the largest proportion of the vote in a constituency wins the seat and other candidates do not win anything; in the latter, seats are allotted according to a party's proportion of the vote in the whole country, so even if a party comes second in a number of constituencies, it will still win some seats. The former system aims to give a solid majority to one party while the latter aims to give a fair distribution of seats to the parties. The Italian system is an attempt to obtain the best of both systems.

The Economy

"An untouchable and sacred state institution, on a par with royalty, the church, a regime."

Italian dictator Benito Mussolini on the Fiat automobile company

During the second half of the 20th century, Italy moved from being a largely agricultural country to being one of the world's major economic powers. This was achieved through its inventive business people, designers, and engineers, who have adapted quickly to changes in world markets. Italy is famous for many different products, ranging from clothing and leather goods to agricultural products, although its main exports are now industrial machinery and textiles. The country is unusual among major industrial nations in that much of its industry is based on smaller family firms that export quality products with a specific market. In recent years the country has made huge strides to overcome its public debt and problems with inflation in order to meet the criteria needed for entry into the common European currency, the euro, which will replace the Italian lira in 2002.

FACT FILE

• Italy has the sixth-largest economy in the world.

• Italy is the fourth most popular tourist destination in terms of arrivals, after France, the United States, and Spain. In terms of tourist income, Italy is second, reflecting the high spending of visitors to Italy.

• Italy is the world's largest exporter of tomatoes and tomato products.

• More than half of Italian industry is concentrated in a triangle formed by the northern cities of Turin, Milan, and Genoa.

• Italy is the world's fifth-largest producer of both fruit and vegetables.

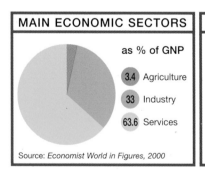

MAIN ECONOMIC SECTORS

as % of GNP

3.4	Agriculture
33	Industry
63.6	Services

Source: *Economist World in Figures, 2000*

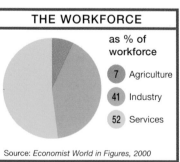

THE WORKFORCE

as % of workforce

7	Agriculture
41	Industry
52	Services

Source: *Economist World in Figures, 2000*

Italy produces more wine than any other country. Even steep terrain is used, split into terraces, like these hills on the Amalfi coast south of Naples.

MAIN TRADING PARTNERS

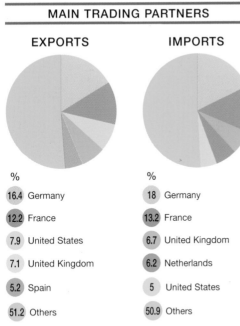

EXPORTS		IMPORTS	
%		%	
16.4	Germany	18	Germany
12.2	France	13.2	France
7.9	United States	6.7	United Kingdom
7.1	United Kingdom	6.2	Netherlands
5.2	Spain	5	United States
51.2	Others	50.9	Others

Source: *Economist World in Figures, 2000*

EXPORTS ($bn)		IMPORTS ($bn)	
● Engineering products	85	● Engineering products	49.0
● Textiles and clothing	39.3	● Chemicals	29.2
● Transport equipment	23.4	● Transport equipment & parts	25.2
● Chemicals	20.5	● Energy products	21.9
● Food and drink	9.8		
Total (including others)	238.3	Total (including others)	208.3

Source: *Economist World in Figures, 2000*

Large and Small Business

Italy is unusual for a modern industrial country, because it has many small and medium-sized companies and relatively few large ones. About 90 percent of Italian companies employ between 11 and 500 people, often with fewer rather than more workers.

Smaller businesses are often more flexible than some larger companies. When times are hard, they can scale down their activities, and when things get better, they can sometimes respond more quickly to changes in the economy.

Families are important in business. Many of the smaller companies are run by families. Some large industrial groups are strongly identified with the families that founded them, such as the Agnellis who set up the auto giant Fiat in Turin. Some of the smaller companies work directly for the large ones. For example, they may specialize in one product or part of a production process needed by the automobile industry.

Other small businesses are more independent and successfully export their own products to other countries. About 40 percent of companies with fewer than 50 employees depend on exports for the majority of their earnings.

The big companies are mainly concentrated in northern Italy, especially in the area between Milan, Turin, and Genoa. Milan is Italy's financial and industrial center. It is also home to Italy's fashion industry.

Textiles and clothing form Italy's second largest export in terms of revenue. When the European Economic Community (EEC), the first economic association of European countries, was set up in 1957, Italy was one of the original members. In 1993, Italy was one of the 15 countries that formed the European Union, which allowed political cooperation and free trade between its members.

Being a member of the European Union is very important for Italy. The European Union is Italy's largest trading partner. The country sends 55 percent of its exports there, and takes 60 percent of its imports from the European Union. The United States is the next largest export market, making up approximately 8 percent of the total.

EUROPEAN UNION

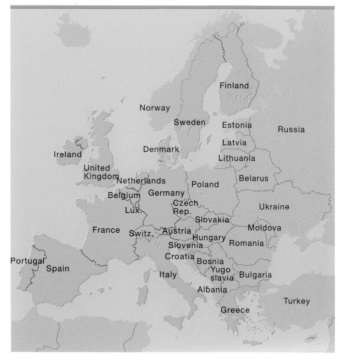

European Union member countries

Non-member Countries

The expansion of the current EU of 15 countries to include several Eastern European countries, such as Poland and the Czech Republic, was the subject of an intergovernmental conference at Nice, France, in December 2000.

North and South

The richest regions of Italy are all in northern and central Italy. Southern Italy generates only about one-fifth of tax revenues, although 35 percent of public spending goes to the south. (Government spending is calculated according to the size of the population.) Twenty-six percent of people in the south are considered poor—those with an income less than half the average income per person—against 9 percent in northern and central Italy.

In 1950 a special fund called the *Cassa del Mezzogiorno* (State Fund for the South) was set up to help develop the south. Money from the fund was used to modernize agriculture, create industrial zones, and improve infrastructure by building 1,240 miles (2,000 km) of super-highways and modernizing ports. Agricultural output doubled within 20 years. Some large corporations, including steel and automobile manufacturers, set up plants in cities like Taranto, Naples, and Bari.

Despite this large investment, the south still has a much higher level of unemployment than the north. The average for the whole country is about 12 percent, but in the south it is 21.7 percent.

Finding a job is especially difficult in the south where 33.8 percent of 15 to 24 year olds are without work. Since many young people go to a university first, then look for their first job, there are high levels of graduates unemployed. In some areas up to 80 percent of people looking for work are graduates.

In northern and central Italy, young people take temporary jobs as a stepping stone to permanent employment. In the south, young job seekers often reject temporary low-status jobs, which are poorly paid, as they worry about not being able to move on to a better job. They look for government jobs, which are permanent, steady, and better paid. For example, up to 20 percent of Sicily's workforce work for the government in universities, government offices, museums, or historic sites.

On the Move

One of the ways in which people escaped from lack of opportunity, especially in the south, was to move away. Between 1861 and 1973, 26 million Italians left Italy. It was only in 1973, for the first time in Italy's recent history, that more Italians returned than left the country.

The first large groups of emigrants left northern Italy in the 1860s, followed later by millions of southerners. Emigrants went to South America, settling in countries like Argentina, Brazil, and Uruguay, but the majority went to live in the United States. After World War II, Italians looked for work in European countries, like Switzerland, France, and Germany.

In the 1950s and 1960s, there was a great wave of migration within Italy. Many people moved from the south to work in the new factories around Milan, Turin, Genoa, and Bologna. There were no language problems and it was easier to take the family along. Even today, young people still move from the poorer regions of the south in search of work.

Farming and Fishing

About 7 percent of Italians work in agriculture. They cultivate the 40 percent of Italy's land area devoted to farming. Many farms are small: about 75 percent cover 12 acres (5 hectares) or less. The larger, more modern farms are mainly in northern and central Italy, especially in the Po Valley. Despite the efforts of the Italian government to improve farming, mountain areas and parts of the south are still fairly unproductive.

One of the most valuable crops is grapes. Most of them are used for making wine. Better wines have the words *Denominazione di Origine Controllata*, or DOC, on the labels. This indicates a good-quality wine which comes from one wine-growing area. Olives are grown mainly in the center and the south. They are also processed to make olive oil. Some of the top quality brands are also categorized as DOC oils. Just like wine, the flavor of olive oil varies from one area to another, depending on the soil and climate conditions.

Other major fruit and vegetable produce includes oranges, lemons, peaches, apples, and tomatoes. Sicily produces about 60 percent of all citrus fruits grown in Italy. Sugar beet is also produced on a wide scale.

A crop not immediately associated with Italy is rice. It is grown in large water-logged fields around

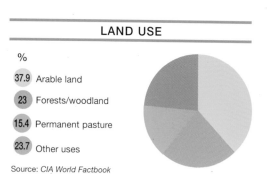

HOW ITALY USES ITS LAND

Cropland
Forest
Pasture
Mountains

Italy makes good use of its available land, although much of its terrain is too rugged for farming.

LAND USE

%	
37.9	Arable land
23	Forests/woodland
15.4	Permanent pasture
23.7	Other uses

Source: *CIA World Factbook*

Men in northern Italy operate an olive press, producing quality olive oil for Italy's export market.

Vercelli and Novara, in northwest Italy. This area accounts for about 60 percent of Italian rice production. Corn and wheat are important grain crops.

There are problems with irrigating food crops. In some areas, especially farther south, there is a shortage of water; in others there are difficulties because of water pollution, or because the available water is too salty.

Cattle are raised for meat and milk, especially in the north and the center. Large numbers of other animals, like pigs, chickens, and sheep, are raised for meat, but the country still has to import some from other countries because Italian people eat more meat than the country's farmers can supply.

Although Italy is surrounded by sea and Italians love to eat fish and seafood, fishing is not a very important economic activity. About half the catch comes from the Adriatic, but fish stocks are low because of the use of drift-nets which catch undersized or young fish before they can mature and breed more. Italian fishing fleets also work farther away in the Mediterranean and even the Atlantic. Around Sicily, tuna, anchovies, and sardines are caught.

Mineral Resources and Energy

Italy has very little oil; what there is mostly lies in the Po Valley, Calabria, and Sicily. There are also some natural gas reserves. The country has to import about 75 percent of its energy requirements, mainly oil and gas from North Africa. The possibility of using nuclear power as a major source of energy supply was abandoned after the Italian people overwhelmingly voted against the idea in a referendum in 1987.

Oil provides about half of the country's energy needs, and about 85 percent of Italian electricity power plants burn oil. About 17 percent of electricity is generated in hydroelectric power plants. These are mostly in the Alps in the north, with some plants in the Apennines.

Many raw materials needed for industrial production are also imported. Some minerals are mined, including mercury, pyrites (a source of sulfur), iron ore, potash, zinc, lead, and salt. One famous mineral export from Italy is the high-quality white marble from quarries in the Apennines at Carrara, in Tuscany. Michelangelo used to come to Carrara to choose blocks for his sculptures (*see* p. 98), and modern sculptors still visit the quarry today.

ENERGY SOURCES

%

80.2 Fossil fuels (coal, gas, oil)

17.3 Hydroelectric power

2.5 Other

Source: *CIA World Fact Book, 1996*

Dependence on imported fossil fuels makes Italy's economy very vulnerable to changes in world oil prices.

Industry

Manufacturing accounts for nearly 20 percent of Italy's GDP (gross domestic product). About 40 percent of Italians work in industry. Machine tools, textile machinery, and industrial robots from the mechanical engineering industry are key exports. The textile and leatherworking sector is also important, producing clothes and fashion accessories for sale around the world.

United Colors

Some Italian companies started small and grew. One of the largest corporations in the textile and clothing sector began as a small company run by the Benetton family. It was based at Ponzano Veneto, in the northeastern province of Treviso. Set up in 1965, it now sells clothes worldwide through a chain of shops. The company began by subcontracting the making of clothes to a number of smaller companies in the local Veneto area, managing the production with sophisticated computerized control of stocks and payment.

Style Leaders

Italians like to look fashionable, even if they are just going out for a stroll or a coffee with friends, or going shopping. Some people are so interested in fashion that they wear only designer labels. They are called *firmati* (signed), because they wear clothes with a designer name. The Italian fashion industry, with its twice-yearly shows, is based around the city of Milan. Famous Italian fashion designers include Gucci, Prada, Versace, Armani, Dolce e Gabbana, and Valentino.

At home Italians like to buy stylish designer furniture or houseware. One company set up by the Alessi family produces a whole range of tableware and kitchenware. Italian design is widely acknowledged as a world leader. This development even extends to the styling of high-performance cars and motorcycles, which are automatically linked with the luxury products of Enzo Ferrari, Ferrucio Lamborghini, Adriano Ducati, and Fabio Taglioni.

Food-processing, based on the agricultural crops grown in Italy, is the country's third-largest industrial sector. Other important industries include petroleum products, automobiles, and chemicals. Electrical products include electronic equipment for business and military use. The nonelectrical goods sector produces domestic appliances, such as refrigerators, washing machines, and dishwashers. The Italian government has a share in many large industrial corporations, including shipyards, steel plants, and automobile plants. It even owns a food-processing company.

The automobile giant Fiat also produces aircraft engines and telecommunications equipment, and has recently developed interests in biological science.

Services

More than 60 percent of Italians work in service industries, especially in retailing, hotels, and restaurants. The government also employs a large number of people; 12 percent of workers have government jobs. The computer software sector employs 162,000 people.

Tourism generates income for many regions of Italy, and is especially welcome in the poorer areas. As many

MAJOR INDUSTRIES

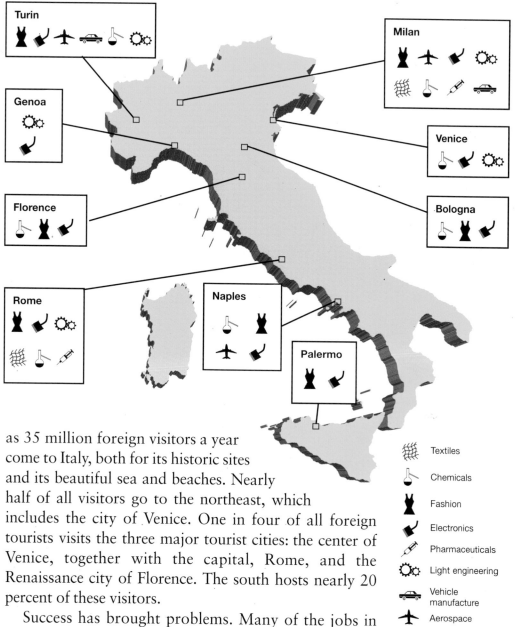

Turin

Milan

Genoa

Venice

Florence

Bologna

Rome

Naples

Palermo

Textiles
Chemicals
Fashion
Electronics
Pharmaceuticals
Light engineering
Vehicle manufacture
Aerospace

as 35 million foreign visitors a year come to Italy, both for its historic sites and its beautiful sea and beaches. Nearly half of all visitors go to the northeast, which includes the city of Venice. One in four of all foreign tourists visits the three major tourist cities: the center of Venice, together with the capital, Rome, and the Renaissance city of Florence. The south hosts nearly 20 percent of these visitors.

Success has brought problems. Many of the jobs in tourism are only seasonal. There is a lot of illegal, unplanned building along coastal areas. Unregulated construction around scenic landscapes like the Bay of Naples, for example, has led to the imposition of more rigid planning controls.

Romans' Holidays

Although more and more Italians travel abroad on vacation every year—spending over $16 billion abroad in 1997—83 percent still choose to visit resorts in their own country. Italians have long vacations in comparison to other European countries, between four and six weeks a year, taken as longer trips of two weeks or more in summer and short breaks at other times of the year.

In August some factories shut down for a month and many shops also close for the period, especially around the 15th of August, the Feast of the Assumption, which is called *Ferragosto.* Traditionally, this is the period when the Italian population heads for the beaches. Large cities like Milan and Turin are less busy, because so many residents have left to go to beach resorts. In the busiest summer season, a large resort like Rimini on the Adriatic Coast has up to two million visitors from Italy and other parts of Europe. Some coastal towns make 90 percent of their income during this one month. The fact that many Italians take their vacation at the same time can cause large traffic jams on the main highways, and seats on trains are hard to find. The *rientro* (literally "reentrance"), when Italians return to the cities, also causes major problems.

COMMUNICATIONS AND TRANSPORTATION

The telephone system in Italy is modern and fully automated. There are over 26 million telephones in the country. As in most of western Europe, cellular phones are also very popular.

The historic centers of many Italian cities are not very well adapted for large-scale traffic. People use small automobiles and motorbikes to get around. Workers and students also use trains to commute into larger towns and cities. Travel to work or school may also be by bus or in the major cities by streetcar.

Road Transportation

Italy's road network is extensive and efficient. The highway system extends for 189,340 miles (305,388 km), most of which is paved. The excellent *autostrada* (super-highway) system covers more than 4,302 miles (6,940 km) and links all the main Italian cities. Automobile travelers pay expensive tolls to use the *autostrada*. The system was massively expanded during the period from 1955 to 1975, partly spurred on by the rapid increase in car ownership during this time. Italy's highways were largely built by private companies employed by the government and building has been funded by highway tolls. Freight is largely carried by road, due to the slow expansion of the railroad network during the 20th century. Automobile ownership in Italy is high and this has caused problems of pollution and congestion in the country's city centers. Some cities, such as Milan and Bologna,

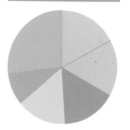

MAIN FOREIGN ARRIVALS

%

17	Switzerland
16	France
16	Germany
15	Yugoslavia
9	Austria
27	Others

Source: Government of Italy, 1997

Made in Italy

The Italian people have been famous for many inventions. The *pantelgrafo*, a forerunner of the fax machine, was invented by Giovanni Caselli in 1856. Composer Gioacchino Rossini even sent a musical score by *pantelgrafo*. In 1871, Antonio Meucci designed a telephone but he could not afford to renew the patent, so Alexander Graham Bell was able to patent his telephone in 1876. Nobel-prizewinning physicist Guglielmo Marconi (1874–1937) sent the first radio signals across the Atlantic in 1901.

The world's first superhighway was the *autostrada* between Milan and Varese, which was opened in 1924.

TRANSPORTATION

Italy's best communications lie around the industrialized centers of the northern cities. In the south, public works projects suffer from funds being siphoned off through local corruption. Major national highways include the *Autostrada del Sole*, the highway that links Milan with Rome and the south. Alpine tunnels link northern Italy with the rest of Europe, and an efficiently maintained system of roads links the country's major centers.

Major highways
Railroad
Major airport
Navigable river

During the fascist period, Mussolini was famous for making the railroads function efficiently. Today, people say that Italian trains have not run on time since!

close to private motor vehicles when pollution exceeds a certain level. This has led to attempts to introduce cleaner fuels for both public and private vehicles.

Rail travel in Italy is inexpensive when compared with most European countries. Most of the railroad network, which extends for 12,092 miles (19,503 km), is state owned and heavily subsidized. Although the network is extensive, Italian trains are famous for their late arrivals. One train often waits for another before departing and thus causes a string of delays. A trip from Milan to Rome takes about 4 hours; Rome to Naples takes 1 hour 45 minutes.

Although water transportation has been important in Italy's history, there are few internal waterways in the country. The Po River is the country's only navigable internal waterway. Italy has many merchant ships. For transportation of goods around Italy by sea the main ports are Genoa, Naples, Civitavecchia, Taranto, Augusta (Sicily), and Olbia (Sardinia). Trieste, Genoa, and Taranto are major ports for international trade.

The national airline, Alitalia, flies to many international destinations; in addition, charter airlines run services between Italy and other major European cities. There are major international airports at Rome, Fiumicino (Leonardo da Vinci) and Milan, Malpensa.

When Greece, Spain, and Portugal joined the European Union in the late 1980s, Italy faced fierce competition for its Mediterranean agricultural products, such as olive oil and fruit.

First or Second Capital?

Rome may be Italy's political capital, but there is no doubt that the more serious and hardworking northern city of Milan is in every way the country's industrial center. The Romans claim that the *Milanesi* are humorless and work too hard, while the Lombardians retort that the success of their industry—producing 30 percent of the country's tax revenues—subsidizes the capital.

For centuries Milan was considered the capital of Italy by its foreign rulers—Charlemagne came here to be crowned—and it still shares extensive links with northern Europe, both cultural, through industry, and through its excellent transportation links. Situated at the center of the Po Valley, Italy's industrial heartland, Milan is also the hub for a complex north Italian transportation network. It has the country's largest stock market and is the city where north European companies come to trade. In addition it is the acknowledged center of Europe's design industry and in terms of earnings from fashion outstrips Paris. Other major industries in the region include vehicle production, electrical appliances (particularly domestic appliances), engineering components, and chemicals. Milan is also the center of Italy's internet industry, although most other media are centered in Rome, including the state companies of the RAI (see p. 105).

The downside to Milan's economic miracle is the urban sprawl that surrounds the ancient city center, and the smog that often makes the air hard to breathe. Restrictions are sometimes imposed to limit the number of motor vehicles entering the city, and face masks are donned by the city's traffic police.

Arts and Living

*"There is no end. There is no beginning.
There is only the infinite passion of life."*

Italian film director Federico Fellini

Italy has one of the richest cultural heritages of any modern nation. Its position at the center of the Roman empire and then as the home of the Catholic church made it a center of work for artists. This encouraged the development of many different art forms. Historically, the peninsula's competing city-states fought to outdo each other in the lavishness of their decoration as they did in the ferocity of their military campaigns. This history gave the region a concentration of artistic riches unequaled in the Western world. Visitors to Italy are often astounded by the sheer accumulation of history and cultural artifacts that are found in even the smallest towns.

This inheritance from the past lives on in much of Italian life. Many people still live in buildings that are hundreds of years old, and local customs persist at almost every level, in the language, cuisine, and *modi di fare,* or behavior, of each region.

There have been attempts to break with the past—notably during the fascist period. Contemporary Italy is influenced by the industrial culture of its northern towns. The country's leadership in world design, fashion, and engineering affects much of its modern cultural life, and throughout Italian daily life there is a strong feeling for the visual arts. Today Italy is fortunate to mix the best of its historic past with the hi-tech economy and liberal institutions of a modern European state.

Italy's cuisine is based on a combination of traditionally separate regions. Food in the north is generally heavier, while that of the south is spicier and sweeter.

THE ARTS

Italy is unique in the Western world in that its artistic past has almost continually influenced the works of the present. It is possible to trace a tradition of rational nonreligious culture that stretched from classical times to the Renaissance—values that are still visible in contemporary Italian society.

Architecture

Italy is full of historic architecture, some of it in ruins, some perfectly preserved. Most Italian cities have historic centers, ringed by suburbs of modern apartment blocks.

This first-century fresco from a Roman villa at Pompeii displays a fine command of perspective. The Romans were strongly influenced by earlier Greek techniques.

Although great Roman temples were built of marble and stone, others were built of brick or concrete. Styles were inspired by the straight beams and columns of ancient Greek buildings, but also by the construction techniques of the Etruscans, who used arches and vaults. The Romans discovered that it was quicker to build using small stones and rubble held together with concrete than to cut large stone blocks and fit them together. Concrete was made from lime and fine volcanic earth. Stone was often used as a facing material to cover the wall underneath. Columns were decorated at the top with carved capitals.

Roman styles were revived with Romanesque architecture in the 11th century. Churches had round arched windows, with carving on external walls. Later, as building techniques improved, Gothic churches were built higher with tall, slim windows. Inside the impression was of light and a feeling of movement upward emphasized by slender columns and pointed arches. Perhaps the most famous example of Italian Gothic is Milan Cathedral.

During the Renaissance, architects looked to ancient Greece for inspiration. When designing the dome of the cathedral in Florence, Filippo Brunelleschi (1377–1446) made a structure with simple lines. Other well-known Renaissance architects were Donato Bramante (1444–1514), who built the *tempietto* (small church) in Rome, which allegedly covered the site of St. Peter's martyrdom; Leon Battista Alberti (1404–1472), who wrote a famous treatise on perspective; and Andrea Palladio (1508–1580), whose *Four Books of Architecture* had a major influence on European architecture for over 200 years.

Baroque was the style of the 17th and 18th centuries. It was very elaborate, with façades filled with curves, carvings, and statues. During this time Gian Lorenzo Bernini designed St. Peter's Square in Rome (*see* p. 39).

Italians also enjoy good modern design. Italian architecture and the arts generally fell into decline after the late 18th century due to repeated invasions by foreign powers. A revival of sorts occurred in architecture under the fascists in the 20th century, with important buildings including the station at Florence (1933–1935) and the Casa del Fascio in Como (1932–1936). More recently, working with Pier Luigi Nervi (1891–1979) as structural engineer, Gio Ponti (1891–1979) is well-known for the

Pier Luigi Nervi developed the use of ferro cemento, a mixture of steel mesh and cement that enabled him to construct vast but solid structures, such as this Tourist Pavilion built near Milan in 1960.

Pirelli Building in Milan. Nervi often used reinforced concrete in his designs, including stadiums for the 1960 Rome Olympics and San Francisco Cathedral in the United States. Perhaps the most famous contemporary Italian architect is Renzo Piano (born 1937), responsible for the Pompidou Center in Paris (1972–1976, with Richard Rogers) and for Kansai Airport in Japan (1994).

Painting and Sculpture

In the late Middle Ages talented artists were busy all over Italy, creating artworks for rich noblemen, bishops, and the pope. Much of this work was produced for the church, and paintings usually showed scenes from the Christian religion or from ancient legend.

Their work was important in the developments in art. Giotto (1266–1337) broke away from the stiff lines of Byzantine and Gothic art. In the frescoes he painted in Assisi, Padua, and Florence the figures are softer and more natural.

During the Renaissance period (from the 1350s onward)

Copies of Ghiberti's groundbreaking designs for the Baptistery Doors still adorn the building, which stands opposite the cathedral in the center of Florence.

new techniques brought great changes to painting. Artists began to understand the use of perspective, which gave a feeling of depth to pictures. In sculpture Lorenzo Ghiberti (1378–1455) inspired others with his bronze panels for the Gate of Paradise on the Baptistery in Florence. Another sculptor, Donatello (1386–1466), modeled natural-looking statues, including a bronze of the biblical hero David and the largest bronze statue of a rider on a horse made since Roman times, called *Gattamelata*.

Fifteenth-century painters like Masaccio (1401–1428), Paolo Uccello (1397–1475), Piero della Francesca (1420–1492), and Andrea Mantegna (1431–1506) carefully studied the structure and proportions of the human body, so that they could make their paintings more realistic. They lived and worked in flourishing commercial centers like Florence, Venice, Mantua, Arezzo, and Perugia, traveling to other cities to complete commissions for clients.

In the following century, master painters like Titian (1490–1576), Tintoretto (1518–1594), and Veronese (1528–1588) worked in Venice, creating artworks for the many churches in the city and for the head of the Venetian state, the doge. Raphael (1483–1520), who spent many years working for the pope in Rome, painted calm, balanced pictures. He was an excellent portrait painter, and took care to perfect the details, even hands. Painting hands can be difficult, and some painters charged more for including them in portraits. Raphael used the hands to show more about the personality of the person he was painting.

Sandro Botticelli's masterpiece the Primavera (Spring) shows various allegorical figures. From left to right they are: Mercury, messenger of the gods; the Three Graces; Venus, representing humanity; Flora, goddess of flowers and spring; the earth nymph Chloris; and Zephyr, the west wind.

Developments in Painting

In medieval Italy there were no art schools. To learn about painting, boys became apprentices, and worked in the artist's workshop. There was a lot to learn. Up until the 15th century, paintings were done on wood or on wet plaster (a technique known as fresco). The apprentices put a coat of fine plaster on the wall. An outline of the fresco was marked out with charcoal. Then the artist had to work quickly to finish the fresco, before the plaster dried.

The paint colors—pigments mixed with egg yolk and water—sank into the wet plaster and merged with it. Once dry, the painting could not be changed.

In the late 1400s, artists started to work on canvas stretched over a wooden frame. It was easy to move, and did not crack when the temperature changed. Artists found that adding linseed or walnut oil to color pigments made a smooth, shiny paste. This oil paint dried slowly, allowing changes to be made.

Michelangelo's Pietà, *representing the Virgin Mary and the dead Christ, was sculpted when the artist was only 25 years old.*

Two of the world's great artists emerged in the 15th century: Leonardo da Vinci and Michelangelo. Both were good examples of Renaissance men—a term given to individuals who worked in more than one discipline and were talented in several different directions. The abundance of learning and culture during this period also encouraged people to explore new directions in terms of artistic techniques and the sciences.

Leonardo (1452–1519) was not only a very talented artist but also a scientific genius. In his masterpieces, like the *Last Supper* and the *Mona Lisa*, he created some of the most famous depictions of the human form. As a military engineer and architect, he designed many extraordinary machines, including what looked like an early version of a helicopter. His other interests included anatomy, botany, geology, hydraulics, and mechanics. Although Leonardo had worked mainly in Milan, he died at the court of the French king, Francis I, for whom he was chief painter and architect from 1516.

Michelangelo Buonarotti (1475–1564) worked for the Medici family in Florence and then for the pope in Rome. He is famous for his expressive sculptures, especially his *David*. This statue, sculpted out of white marble, stands 12 feet (4m) high, twice human size. Michelangelo also spent years painting scenes from the Bible on the ceiling of the Sistine Chapel in the Vatican, and wrote poetry. At the end of his life he was chief architect on St. Peter's in Rome.

The development of Michelangelo's painting and sculptural style into a freer line was a forerunner of the Baroque style of the 16th and 17th centuries, a fine example of which is the ceiling fresco of Sant' Ignazio in Rome. Two important artists of this period were Annibale Carracci (1560–1609) and Caravaggio (1571–1610). In sculpture, Gian Lorenzo Bernini (1589–1680) produced lavish and dramatic compositions for the churches of Rome. In the mid-18th century, Italian artists worked in the courts of France and Germany. Giovanni Battista Tiepolo (1696–1770) produced dramatic Baroque frescos, while Francesco Guardi (1712–1793) and Canaletto (1697–1768) were chiefly patronized by foreign clients visiting their native Venice.

During the late 18th and early 19th centuries, Italian artists looked backward to their illustrious past and the incentives for creative art moved to France and northern Europe. From the late 19th century, the Italian *Divisionisti* depicted the play of light and shade on realistic subjects, often depicting

The Reformation and the emergence of Protestantism in northern Europe posed a real threat to the Catholic church in Rome. As a result, the popes of the 16th century embarked on a Counter-Reformation, and used the work of Renaissance artists to glorify Rome and the Catholic church.

Artemesia Gentileschi

The Neapolitan Artemesia Gentileschi (1593–1652) was a rare example of a successful 17th-century woman painter. She portrayed realistic portraits and biblical scenes in rich colors, using deep shadow and dramatic perspective. The daughter of another successful painter, Orazio Gentileschi, she was influenced by Caravaggio's use of light and shade. She showed herself to be an astute businesswoman, carving a successful career in painting the Spanish nobles who ruled Naples at the time.

Giorgio di Chirico

Born in Vollos, Greece, in 1888 of Italian parents, de Chirico studied at the Academy of Fine Arts in Munich. His early work was quickly linked with the Surrealist movement. The Surrealists placed emphasis on the imagination and the disturbing placement of unrelated objects and ideas. Di Chirico's paintings featured deserted, shadowy piazzas, rendered in flat color and with unconventional elements, such as a banana and a marble bust. He moved to Paris in 1911 and was supported by Picasso and Guillaume Apollinaire. After 1919, his painting became more formal and academic and he disowned his earlier work (now considered his best). Later he settled in Rome and worked intermittently until his death in 1978.

Because Dante's *Divine Comedy* was written in the Florentine dialect that later formed the basis of modern Italian, the work is often considered the first work of Italian literature. It has a similar importance in Italian to Shakespeare's work in English.

workers or peasants in work that echoed that of the French Impressionists. Perhaps foremost among the *Divisionisti* was Angelo Morbelli (1853–1919). In the early 20th century the most prominent Italian movement was that of Futurism. Launched in Milan in 1908 by the poet Emilio Marinetti (1876– 1944), this movement marked a deliberate break with Italy's artistic past: "Burn the museums! Drain the canals of Venice!" Marinetti declared. The movement took as its subject the depiction of speed, and of the new age of machines. Figures were often shown in movement. Futurist painting and sculpture frequently depicted events happening simultaneously. In the 1920s and 1930s Futurism was revived under the dictatorship of Mussolini. In the 1960s another important Italian movement was that of *Arte Povera* (Art of the Poor). Inspired by the ideals of equality popular during this period, the movement used "found" or discarded materials to create sculptures and other artworks, and for the first time used modern materials such as plastics and objects of mass production.

Literature

Although as many as 14 languages developed in Italy from Latin, up until around 1200 it was not thought appropriate to write literature in these languages. Many poems were composed in Sicilian at the court of Frederic II. Saint Francis of Assisi (1182–1226) wrote his *Canticle of the Sun* in a local dialect, but Latin was still the proper language for educated people to write in. The Florentine poet, Dante Alighieri (1265–1321), wrote a book explaining why he supported writing in local languages, but wrote it in Latin. Later, his long poem *The Divine Comedy*, became the first major work of literature to be written in a local dialect. Dante wrote in the dialect derived from Latin that was spoken by the Florentines. This dialect later developed into what we know today as Italian.

The Divine Comedy has three sections: Hell, Purgatory, and Paradise. Dante makes an imaginary journey through Hell, meeting people from Italy's past, and friends and enemies. The journey is also about the progress of a soul toward God and human progress to peace on earth.

The Renaissance provided a great flowering of literature in Italy as it did in the other arts. The most important writer of this period was Giovanni Boccaccio (1313–1375), whose *Decameron*, a series of stories related by individuals escaping the plague in Florence, was a major influence on the English poet Geoffrey Chaucer.

Later, Alessandro Manzoni (1785–1873), a leading writer of the Romantic period, also came from Tuscany. His historical novel *The Betrothed* (1827) is very important, because the way it was written became a model for modern Italian novels. The book is about how two poor peasants, Renzo and Lucia, marry despite the attempts of the local lord to stop them. Most Italians study this book in high school. Giovanni Verga (1840–1922) wrote about the people of Sicily. He described the life of farmworkers in a very realistic way. Author Grazia Deledda (1871–1936) brought to life the people of

The Florentine writer Dante is shown outside the walls of his native town (the dome of the cathedral is visible on the right). To the left are the circles of hell described in his Divine Comedy.

Sardinia. For her short stories and novels she was awarded the Nobel Prize for Literature in 1926. Italo Svevo (1861–1928) and Oscar Pirandello (1867–1936) brought the influences of psychology and modernism to the Italian novel and drama at the beginning of the 20th century, while Ignazio Silone (1900–1978) wrote about the harsh life of southern Italians and the need for reforms. Later Italian novelists of note include Italo Calvino (1923–85) and Umberto Eco (born 1932). The latter, a university professor from Bologna, achieved international fame with his first novel *Il Nome della Rosa* (*The Name of the Rose*), which was made into a film starring Sean Connery.

Music

The notation that we use for music was invented in Italy and many of the terms that we use to describe the way a piece of music should be played—such as *allegro* (fast or happy), *fortissimo* (very loud), and *crescendo* (increasing in volume)—are taken from Italian. The country

Opened in 1778, Milan's La Scala is one of the world's great opera houses. The first work performed here was by Antonio Salieri, portrayed in the film Amadeus *as Mozart's great rival.*

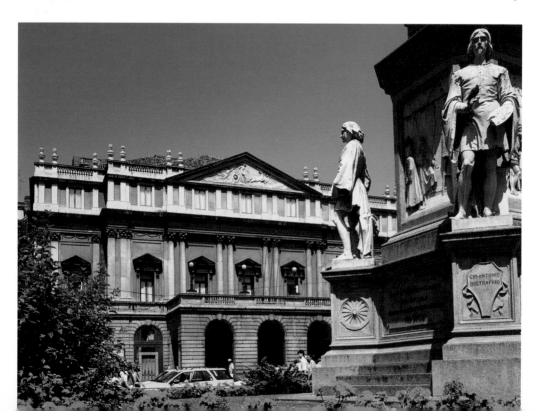

also played a central role in the development of musical forms. The first musical score printed with movable type was created in Venice in the 16th century. Opera began in Florence at the end of the 16th century and spread to Venice, where the first opera theater opened in 1637. Perhaps the most famous Italian composer from this period is Claudio Monteverdi (1567–1643), although his fame was soon superseded by that of the Venetian Antonio Vivaldi (1675–1741), whose *Four Seasons* is still much performed. However, it was in the 19th century that Italian composers dominated the modern opera with the light operas of Rossini (1792–1868, *The Barber of Seville* (1816), *William Tell* (1829)), Donizetti (1797–1848, *Lucrezia Borgia* (1833)), Bellini (1801–1835, *Norma* (1831)), Puccini (1858–1924), *La Bohème* (1896), *Tosca* (1900), *Madama Butterfly* (1904)), and, above all, Giuseppe Verdi (1813–1901, *La Traviata* (1853), *Aïda* (1871)). These works achieved an importance in the history of opera that has never been surpassed.

Born in Parma in northern Italy in 1935, the tenor Luciano Pavarotti has achieved international fame both with public performances and with a series of successful recordings.

The Movies

Although the Italian film industry produced some notable spectacular films in the silent era, by the early 1930s, Italian studios were approaching bankruptcy. The industry was placed under government control by Mussolini in the late 1930s and early 1940s and a vast film complex called Cinecittà was built outside Rome by the fascists. In its first years Cinecittà was tainted by its production of fascist propaganda films, works that became increasingly

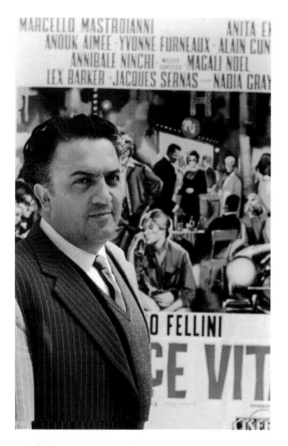

The director Federico Fellini, who was born at Rimini in northeast Italy, stands in front of a poster for his most famous film La Dolce Vita.

important with Italy's entrance into World War II. Later, however, the studios became the center of the Italian film industry. Postwar Italian film was dominated by a movement known as neorealism, which took a direct and unsentimental look at Italian life. Perhaps most striking among the work of this period is Roberto Rossellini's (1906–1977) *Roma Città Aperta* (*Rome Open City*, 1945) and *Germania Anno Zero* (*Germany Year Zero*, 1947), both of which show conditions in postwar Europe. Other major talents of neorealism were Luchino Visconti (1906–1976) and Vittorio De Sica. De Sica's 1948 *Ladri di Biciclette* (*Bicycle Thieves*) has become a classic of European cinema.

It was, however, in the 1960s that Italian film achieved its greatest success, with Cinecittà becoming known as the Hollywood of Europe. Rome itself became a center of the international jet set as the economy boomed. The scene was portrayed by Federico Fellini (1920–1994) in his *La Dolce Vita* (1960), the first of a series of very stylish films starring the actor Marcello Mastroianni (1924–1996). Mastroianni was the first of a number of Italian actors, including Sophia Loren (born 1934) and Gina Lollobrigida (born 1927), to achieve truly international fame. Other notable directors of the 1960s were Pier Paolo Pasolini (1922–1975) and Michelangelo Antonioni (born 1912). The 1970s saw the emergence of another major director in the figure of Bernardo Bertolucci (born 1941), whose *Last Tango in Paris* (1972) starred Marlon Brando. Bertolucci's *The*

Last Emperor (1987), which depicted the life of the last emperor of China, won eight Oscars. More recently the sentimental *Cinema Paradiso* (1988), *Il Postino* (*The Postman*, 1994), and *La Vita è Bella* (*Life is Beautiful*, 1997) have achieved international fame, the latter winning an Oscar for its director and star, Roberto Beningni (born 1952).

The Media

There are three main state TV channels called the RAI. Traditionally each of these has been associated with a specific political party. Cable and satellite stations are also numerous. The largest media conglomerate in Italy is Silvio Berlusconi's Finivest, which owns Canale 5.

Important national daily papers include *Corriere della Sera (Evening Courier), La Stampa (The Press),* and *La Repubblica (The Republic)*. In addition to watching sports on TV, fans love to read about it. There are three newspapers and 15 magazines dedicated to

Newspaper stands at main stations and town centers sell a variety of partworks (books split into several parts) as well as the usual magazines and newspapers.

sports reporting. The best-selling title, *Il Corriere dello Sport*, sells 573,000 copies a day compared to a big circulation national paper like *Corriere della Sera*, which sells around 874,000 copies. The Communist Party's national newspaper, *L'Unità (Unity)*, folded in the late 1990s.

DAILY LIFE

Life in Italy is usually centered around the family, and people often rely on family members to help them in difficult times. Most young people still live at home until they marry. Seventy percent of men remain living at home with their parents until they are 35. Italian men have a reputation of liking to be spoiled by their mothers, and having all their meals cooked and their washing done. This can cause problems later when they marry, because their wives are not prepared to do all this work for their husbands, especially if they work themselves.

Getting married is still important in Italy, but fewer and fewer children are being born. In the 1960s it was

Italian cafés serve a variety of coffees, light snacks, and some alcoholic drinks. They charge extra for a seat and many people will drink standing up at the bar rather than pay the extra cost.

How to Say...

In general, Italian is written exactly as it is spoken and is an easy language for English speakers to learn. Double consonants indicate a longer sound.

Please	*Per favore* (PURR fav-OR-ay)	**Numbers**	
Thank you	*Grazie* (GRAR-zee-ay)	One	*Uno* (OO-no)
Yes	*Sì* (SEE)	Two	*Due* (DOO-ay)
No	*No* (NOH)	Three	*Tre* (TRAY)
Hello	*Buongiorno* (BWON-JEE-OR-noh)	Four	*Quattro* (KWOT-roh)
		Five	*Cinque* (CHING-kway)
Goodbye	*Arrivederci* (aree-ve-DER-chee)	Six	*Sei* (SAY)
		Seven	*Sette* (SETT-ay)
Good evening	*Buona sera* (BWONA-SER-ah)	Eight	*Otto* (OTT-oh)
		Nine	*Nove* (NOH-vay)
Good night	*Buona notte* (BWONA-NOT-ay	Ten	*Dieci* (dee-YAY-chee)

		Days of the week	
How are you?	*Come stai?* (KOM-ay STY) (informal); *Come sta?* (KOM-ay-STA) (formal)	Sunday	*Domenica* (doh-MEN-icah)
		Monday	*Lunedi* (LOON-edee)
		Tuesday	*Martedi* (MAR-tedee)
I understand	*Ho capito* (OH-ka-PEE-toh)	Wednesday	*Mercoledi* (MER-cole-dee)
		Thursday	*Giovedi* (JO-veh-dee)
I don't understand	*Non ho capito* (NON-OH-ka-PEE-toh)	Friday	*Venerdi* (VEN-er-dee)
		Saturday	*Sabato* (SAB-at-oh)

common to find families with three or four children. Now Italy has the fifth-lowest birthrate in the world (behind Bulgaria, Latvia, the Czech Republic, and Estonia), and most families have only one child. If the birthrate continues as it is at present, by 2050 the current Italian population of 57 million will have dropped to 41 million. Women are waiting longer to have children for career or economic reasons. Because of the close connection between the state and the Catholic church, divorce only became legal in Italy in 1971 and Italy's divorce rate is among the lowest in the world.

EDUCATIONAL
ATTENDANCE

Further (university)	41%
Secondary (middle) school	88%
Primary	98%

Source: Government of Italy, 1998

All Italian men over 18 years of age may be called up for military service of a year in the army or air force, or 18 months in the Italian navy. Recruits also serve in the *carabinieri*, a type of local police force charged with keeping the peace and controlling minor offenses.

Education

Italian children attend school between the ages of six and 16. The school year runs from September to the end of June. Students attend classes from 8 or 8:30 A.M. until around 1:30 or 2 P.M.

Elementary-school students must have had their sixth birthday before they can start school. Before that, from the age of three to five, they often attend kindergarten. After five years at elementary school, students move on to secondary school at the age of 11. *Scuola media* ("middle school") lasts three years. The subjects that students cover are Italian, history and civic education, geography, math, science, a foreign language, and art. For those who want to study further at college, there are another five years of study. Students can choose from arts-based or science-oriented courses at a *liceo* or college, specialized vocational instruction at technical schools, or teacher training.

If students do not get good marks at the end of a school year, they are not allowed to go on to the next year. On average, 20.5 percent of boys and 11.6 per cent of girls have to repeat a year.

All students who have a *maturità* (high-school) diploma can attend a university. Undergraduate degree courses at a university can last between four (for law or philosophy) and six years (for medicine). Some subjects are so popular that the number of students has been limited by entrance tests. Tuition fees are relatively low, but students do not receive grants for living expenses. Some Italian students study and work part-time and take a long time to finish their degrees.

Religion

Most Italians—84 percent—would call themselves Catholics. The Catholic church and the papacy have had a huge influence on the cultural life of Italy and social attitudes in the country have been shaped largely by the church. Despite this, only one in three Italians goes to mass every Sunday. Fewer young people are coming forward to become priests or nuns. Only a third of priests are under 50 years of age; 44 per cent are between 50 and 60.

In many communities the parish priest still has an important role. He gives parishioners spiritual comfort, but also has many contacts through the community which enable him to help with jobs or other practical matters.

Some people, who are disappointed with traditional Catholic worship, look for spiritual inspiration elsewhere. The second-largest relgous group is Protestant, including the Lutherans of the German-speaking communities of the northeast. There is a small Muslim community in the south of Italy and in some cities of the north, mostly originating in the immigrant communities from northern Africa. In addition, Italy has a small Jewish population. Despite Italy's fascist past, the Jewish community has been treated much better by the ordinary Italian people than in many other parts of Europe.

Annual processions with effigies of saints are common in Italy. Here a figure of San Antonio di Padova is carried through the streets of Rome.

Celebrations

There are many religious festivals in Italy as well as other public holidays. If the holiday falls on a Tuesday or a Thursday, people usually take extra time off on Friday or Monday. They call the extended holiday *il ponte* ("the bridge").

Christmas in Italy is a two-day holiday, Christmas Day and St. Stephen's Day on December 26. Panettone, a light traditional cake with dried fruit, is eaten at

National holidays	
January 1	New Year's Day
January 6	Epiphany
April	Easter Monday
April 25	Liberation Day
May 1	Labor Day
August 15	Feast of the Assumption
November 1	All Saints' Day
December 8	Feast of the Immaculate Conception
December 25	Christmas Day
December 26	St. Stephen's Day

HOW ITALIANS SPEND THEIR MONEY

%

26.3 Housing

19.4 Food

17.3 Transportation

6.7 Clothing

6.0 Leisure

24.3 Other

Source: Italian National Statistical Institute, 1998

During the first weekend of May, pilgrims in the southern town of Bari follow a boat out to sea carrying an image of San Nicola. The pilgrims then hold a ceremony out at sea. The pilgrimage is in honor of the 47 sailors who are believed to have saved the saint's life.

Christmastime. The New Year holiday is January 1. Epiphany (January 6) celebrates the arrival of the Three Kings, and can be another time for giving gifts. Easter is celebrated on Easter Sunday, and the following Monday is also a holiday. Assumption on August 15 honors the Virgin Mary and falls when most people are on vacation for the month of August.

All Saints' Day on November 1 is a somber occasion when people remember family members or friends who have died. The Feast of the Immaculate Conception on December 8 celebrates the time when the Virgin Mary was told her child would be the Son of God.

Two nonreligious public holidays come close together: Liberation Day on April 25 and Labor Day on May 1. Liberation Day marks the surrender of the German and Italian fascist soldiers in World War II.

In addition to these holidays each Italian region has its own special festivals. Towns and villages honor their patron saint with processions and fireworks. Some celebrations go back many centuries. In Siena a horserace called the Palio is held, named after the banner which the winning rider receives. It dates back to the Middle Ages and is held every July 2 and August 16 (*see* opposite).

At the beginning of Lent, the period leading up to Easter, people celebrate carnival by dressing up in costumes and wearing masks. Easter is the most important Christian festival, and there are special Easter celebrations in many regions of Italy, especially in the south.

WHAT DO ITALIANS OWN?

27.9% Microwave Ovens

35.3% Mobile telephones

20% Computer

37% Fax

62.3% Video

28% Dishwasher

Source: Italian National Statistical Institute, 1998

Besides religious festivals, towns hold festivals to celebrate a kind of food or wine. It could be a harvest of cherries, chestnuts, fish, or wine. If it is mushrooms, people try out dishes with mushrooms as a main ingredient.

Food

Italian food is one of the great cuisines of the world. Italians are very proud of their cooking and like to take care about what they prepare. Compared to many countries, there are few foreign restaurants in Italy. Italians even prefer home-grown fast food like pizza or foccaccia, a baked slice of pizza dough flavored with olive oil and herbs, or olives.

To start the day Italians like a coffee. The basic cup of coffee is an espresso, a small cup of strong coffee made with freshly ground coffee beans. It is drunk with sugar but no milk. For breakfast adults may have a slice of bread with jam with an espresso, a cappucino, or a caffelatte (coffee with hot milk).

The Palio

The Palio is a bareback horse-race held in the Tuscan city of Siena twice each summer in honor of the Virgin Mary. Siena is split into 17 different *contrade,* or districts, and ten of these districts compete against each other at each Palio. The *palio* itself is a silk banner, which the winners display in their local headquarters after the race. During the competition the riders tear around Siena's main square, the shell-shaped Piazza del Campo, on a track of packed dirt. A horse without a rider can still win the race and riders are frequently thrown off and injured. Horses are sometimes taken into the local churches for a blessing before the race.

Pizza

You will need:

1 tbsp of dry yeast

1 cup/250ml warm water

3 cups/350g plain wheat flour plus
    more for kneading

1 tbsp of extra virgin olive oil

1 can of chopped tomatoes

1 whole mozzarella sliced

Handful of basil leaves

10 stoned black olives

Dissolve the yeast in the water. Make a mound of the flour and scoop out a bowl in the center. Put the yeast mixture and salt in the bowl. Stir in a circular motion with a fork to mix until a dough forms. Sprinkle a working surface with flour. Put the dough in the center and knead vigorously for about 10 minutes: form a ball, squash flat with the palm of your hand, reform the ball, and so on. Cover the dough with plastic wrap and leave for 1-2 hours until doubled in volume. Turn the dough out, flatten it, and pull out into a circular shape. Cover with the chopped tomatoes and mozzarella slices, sprinkle the other ingredients on top and drizzle with oil. Bake at 425°F (220°C) for ten minutes, then for a further ten minutes at 400°F (200°C).

For lunch in big cities, workers eat in small restaurants like a trattoria, where the food is cooked fresh, or at a *tavola calda* (literally "hot table") with ready-cooked cold roast meat, grilled vegetables, and salads of lettuce, rice, or pasta. In smaller towns people often go home for lunch.

A traditional Italian meal may seem enormous. There can be appetizers of salami and Parma ham or a salad. Next comes the first course of soup, risotto (a rice dish), or pasta, followed by the second course of meat or fish served with vegetables. People finish with some cheese, then fruit or a dessert. Whatever they eat, people often have a glass of good Italian wine to go with the food.

There are many regional dishes, depending on the climate and what grows in the area. In northern Italy people use more butter for cooking than olive oil. Generally the food in northern Italy is heavier, with more meat and dairy produce, rich cheeses and cream and stuffed egg pasta, such as ravioli. Rice is also grown in the north, so there are a lot of recipes for risotto. In the south, pasta is made from wheat alone, with no added eggs and there is greater use of spices—reflecting southern Italy's history of trading with the east. Less meat is also used.

Pasta was introduced from China by Marco Polo, but now people all over Italy eat it. There are more than 600 types, named for their shape. Spaghetti means "little strings," *farfalle* are "butterflies," *conchiglie* are "shells," and *penne* are short, round tubes. Sauces for pasta are varied too. Traditionally spaghetti with tomato sauce comes from Naples, so the sauce is called *napoletana* in Italian. Pesto is associated with Liguria. It is made from basil and pine nuts, an important ingredient that is commonly found in the region.

About two-thirds of Italians live in cities or urban areas, although slightly more people in the south live in the country than in the north. Italians are more likely to buy their homes than to rent them, and families often help their children buy a home when they get married. The downtown areas of Italian cities are full of low-rise historic buildings, some of which may have

In northern Italy Parmesan is used to flavor pasta dishes but in the south, people use *pecorino,* a sharp-tasting sheep's cheese—to give the dish extra taste.

The majority of Italians today live in low-rise apartment houses, such as these on the outskirts of the Tuscan town of Prato.

Out for a stroll

When they have time, Italians like to take an evening stroll, called a *passeggiata* in Italian. Between 6:00 and 8:00 P.M., people go and stroll around the main square or streets of the town, stopping to chat with friends. Sometimes it can be quite noisy, when large groups of people are enthusiastically discussing the latest news about family and friends, sports, or politics.

been divided into offices or apartments. The streets are often narrow, because they were built before cars were invented. Some older city apartment buildings have a central courtyard, with gardens and trees. Farther out from the center, people live in modern apartment houses. An apartment house is often called a *palazzo*, the same word as for a palace.

Before, people who farmed the land in the south used to live in towns and go out to work in the fields. Now, more people have built new homes out on their land.

Some country areas, especially in more remote or mountain areas, have far fewer people living there. Young people prefer to move away to the nearest town or to a large city to find work and a more lively lifestyle.

Sports

Italians can be very passionate about sports, especially soccer, bicycling, and car racing. Professional soccer is a multi-million dollar business in Italy. Many foreign players from other countries in Europe, Latin America, and Africa come to Italy, because they are paid high relocation fees and salaries. In the professional leagues, the best teams play in the *Serie A* (A Series). *Serie-A* teams aim to win the *scudetto*, the shield given to the team that wins the most points during the season. Big cities often have two rival teams: Milan has AC Milan and Inter, Turin has Juventus and Torino, and Rome has Lazio and Roma. Fans identify very strongly with their home teams and the star soccer players playing for their side are idolized by their fans.

Volleyball is very popular in Italy and is often played on the beaches in summer. Italy's national team has won the world championship seven times and regional teams often win international competitions.

Italian teams are also very successful internationally. The national team is known as *gli azzurri* (the blues), because they play in bright blue shirts. Italy has won the World Cup three times, in 1934, 1938, and 1982.

Bicycling is popular with many Italians. Amateur cyclists can be seen out on the roads on weekends. The main Italian road race is the *Giro d'Italia*. Starting in late May or early June, it lasts three weeks and goes all over the peninsula.

Italy has a great tradition in international car racing, with two Formula 1 circuits: one at Monza, north of Milan, where the Italian Grand Prix is held; the other is the San Marino Grand Prix, held on the track at Imola in Emilia-Romagna. Ferrari is a top designer of racing cars, but the team drivers are not always Italian.

Other sports that are popular are traditional ones like outdoor bowling, and basketball and volleyball. Italian competitors have also performed well internationally in yachting events and rowing.

Formula 1 racing cars enter the pit lane at the Imola Grand Prix in central Italy.

The Future

"It [the European Union] will be a deterrent to the darker forces within Italian society."

Head magistrate in the Tangentopoli scandal Antonio di Pietro

Italy today is a thriving democratic country with a rich past and a dynamic future. In spite of this, there are some enduring problems, including the economic differences between the north and the south, organized crime, and inefficient public administration.

Into Europe

The European connection is seen by many Italians as something very important for the future. In opinion surveys many people say that they think that being in the European Union will bring more efficient public administration, better economic growth, and more jobs. They also feel that using one currency, the euro, by all the member-countries of the European Union will also make Italy more competitive and give it more outlets to sell its goods.

They believe that being part of the European Union will force the government to be more disciplined in running the country's finances, because it has to meet targets set by supranational institutions (those operating across several different nations). Even now there is still a large unofficial or "black" economy—illegal smuggling and trading of goods—which is estimated to be around 20 percent of Italy's whole Gross Domestic Product. The government is trying hard to bring this sector into the official system, so it can raise taxes from its income.

The clear waters of Lake Como's picturesque shoreline have recently been the subject of extensive legislation to protect their purity.

FACT FILE

● Italy has one of the most impressive reductions in infant mortality in the Western world. Over the last 25 years rates have effectively been cut by 70 percent.

● The number of internet hosts in Italy (those ending in ".com," ".net," ".org") is low for a country of its size. It lags behind other countries with much smaller populations, such as Finland and the Netherlands, which benefit from having many more English speakers.

● Italy's rates for recycling are among the best in the world. It currently recycles 47 percent of used paper and 54 percent of glass.

In the European Union, individual regions as well as countries feel they have a place and are given financial help from a central fund to which all members contribute. This may help Italy with its north-south divide. It may also limit the power of political groups like the *Lega Nord* (Northern League) which wants northern Italy to become a separate state, so that the north no longer has to contribute to the south (*see* p. 75).

A falling birthrate means that Italy may soon have a population closer to that of Spain than to those of France or Britain, whose size it resembles now.

An Aging Population

At the moment official statistics record more deaths than births in Italy. The average number of children needed per family to keep the population stable is 2.05 children. Italy's average number of children per family is only 1.2. This means that the population is getting older, without enough people being born to take on jobs and make enough money later to support the older citizens. Almost one in five Italians is over the age of 65, and people are usually living longer.

State pensions are generous, and government employees used to be allowed to retire after working for 25 years. Now the system has been changed, people have to contribute for 35 years, or be at least 57 years of age before they can retire. About 10 percent of the Gross Domestic Product goes to pay for pensions, while 5 percent is spent on education. Italy spends much more public money on paying for pensions than it does on children. The regular retirement age is 65 for men and 60 for women.

One section of the population which is increasing is the number of immigrants from North Africa and

Eastern Europe (the main countries are Morocco, the former Yugoslavia, Albania, the Philippines, and the United States). There are about one million official immigrants, but it is estimated there are many more illegal immigrants, perhaps between one and two million. Large groups come from Morocco and Albania, which means that they have languages, religions, and cultures very distinct from that of their host country. In Italy, where people are so aware of differences from just one region to another, Italians are now learning to see themselves as part of a multicultural society. There has recently been discussion in the country about allowing immigrants to build mosques in Italy, a matter of some contention because the Catholic church has been prevented from building churches in some Muslim countries.

The Environment

Fighting pollution poses many problems for Italy today. The huge amount of air pollution generated by cars in cities causes damage to ancient monuments and historic buildings. Bologna and some other cities have banned private cars in some areas. Florence is experimenting with buses that use a mixture of gas and electricity in the historic downtown area, while the smaller city of Ravenna in northeastern Italy uses buses that run on methane.

In some lakes and sections of the northern Adriatic, the discharge of too many fertilizers and detergents led to too many algae being produced. This is a problem especially in the Po Valley, the country's main industrial and agricultural region. Waters flow off the fields from the surrounding farmland bringing with them large amounts of fertilizers and these mix with industrial waste to make the Po River the most polluted in the country. Where the Po flows into the sea, near Ravenna in the northern Adriatic, great masses of algae appear in the water all along the coast. The effect of this problem on Italy's tourist industry and pressure from environmental groups have led to attempts to clean up the area.

Hunters are a powerful lobby group and in 1990 they won a referendum on whether hunting should be banned. Attempts have been made to limit the hunting season but many species, particularly small songbirds, are still at risk.

Almanac

POLITICAL

Country name:
Official long form: Italian Republic
Short form: Italy
Local long form: *Repubblica Italiana*
Local short form: *Italia*

Nationality:
> noun: Italian (s)
> adjective: Italian

Official language: Italian

Capital city: Rome

Type of government: republic

Suffrage (voting rights): everyone 18 years and over

National anthem: *"Fratelli d'Italia"* ("Brothers and Sisters of Italy")

National holiday: April 25 (Liberation Day)

Flag:

GEOGRAPHICAL

Location: Southern Europe; latitudes 39°–47° north and longitudes 7°–18° east

Climate: Alpine in the north, mediterranean in the center and south

Total area: 301,268 square miles (116,293 sq. km)
land: 98%
water: 2%

Coastline: 4,723 miles (7,600 km)

Terrain: mostly mountainous, some plains, coastal lowlands

Highest point: Dufourspitze, 15,203 feet (4,634 m)
Lowest point: no points below sea level

Natural resources: mercury, potash, marble, sulfur, coal, natural gas, and oil

Land use (1993 est.):
arable land: 37.9%
forests and woodland: 23%
permanent pastures: 15%

permanent crops: 10%

other: 14.1%

POPULATION

Population: 57.6 million

Population density: 504 people per
square mile (195 per sq. km)

Population growth rate (2000 est.):
0.09% (due to immigration)

Birthrate (2000 est.): 9.13 births
per 1,000 of the population

Death rate (2000 est.): 9.99 deaths
per 1,000 of the population

Sex ratio (1999 est.): 94 males per
100 females

Total fertility rate (1999 est.): 1.18
children born per woman
in the population

Infant mortality rate (2000 est.):
5.92 deaths per 1,000 live births

Life expectancy at birth (1999 est.):
total population: 79.03 years
male: 75.85 years
female: 82.41 years

Literacy:
total population: 98%

ECONOMY

Currency: Italian lira (Lit.);
1 Lit. = 100 centesimi
The Euro will be used for
all financial transactions
in 2002.

Exchange rate (2000):
$1 = 2,094 Lit.
$1 = 0.94 Euros

Gross national product (1999):
$1.212 trillion (sixth-largest
economy in the world)

Average annual growth rate
(1990–1997): 1.1%

GNP per capita (1999 est.): $21,400

Average annual inflation rate
(1990–1998): 4.1%

Unemployment rate (1999 est.): 11.5%

Exports (1997): $238.3 billion
Imports (1997): $208.3 billion

Foreign aid given (1997): $1.3 billion

Human Development Index
(an index scaled from 0 to 100 combining statistics
indicating adult literacy, years of schooling, life
expectancy, and income levels):

92.2 (U.S. 94.2)

TIME LINE—ITALY

World History

Italian History

50,000 B.C.

c. **40,000** Modern humans—*Homo sapiens sapiens*—emerge.

c. **4000 B.C.** First permanent settlements in Italy.

1500 B.C.

c. **1200 B.C.** Italic and Ligurian tribes settle in northern and central Italy.

8TH CENTURY B.C. Greeks found colonies in southern Italy.

753 B.C. Founding of Rome.

7TH-6TH CENTURIES Peak of Etruscan culture in central Italy.

c. **1100 B.C.** Phoenicians develop the first alphabetic script.

c. **612 B.C.** Fall of the Assyrian empire.

c. **563 B.C.** Birth of Siddharta Gautama, the Buddha.

400 B.C.

396 B.C. Romans defeat Etruscans.

264–146 B.C. Romans defeat Carthaginians in Punic Wars.

327 B.C. Alexander the Great reaches India.

1259 Hanseatic League formed by merchants in Germany.

1206 Delhi Sultanate set up in India.

1096 First Crusade to reclaim Jerusalem begins.

c. 1000 Vikings reach American continent but do not settle.

c. **570** Birth of Mohammed in Mecca.

c. **A.D. 1** Birth of Christ in the Roman province of Judea.

30 B.C. Death of Cleopatra, last of the Ptolemies in Egypt.

1300 onward Rise of city-states in northern and central Italy.

1282 War of Sicilian Vespers leads to Spanish intervention in southern Italy.

1204 Fall of Constantinople to Venice.

1000

A.D. 800 Charlemagne crowned Holy Roman emperor in Rome.

A.D. 560 Lombards invade Italy.

A.D. 476 Fall of the Roman empire.

A.D. 313 Emperor Constantine officially recognizes Christianity.

A.D. 117 Under the Emperor Trajan, Rome reaches its greatest extent.

27 B.C. Augustus becomes the first Roman emperor.

44 B.C. Assassination of Julius Caesar.

50 B.C.

c. 1350

1453 Constantinople falls to the Turks.

1492 Columbus lands in America.

1620 Pilgrim Fathers land in New England.

c. 1750 Industrial Revolution begins in England.

c. 1350–1550 Renaissance leads to rebirth of the arts and classical learning in Europe.

1527 Sack of Rome by Holy Roman emperor, Charles V.

c. 1540 Counter-Reformation aims to reestablish dominance of Catholicism in Europe.

1707 Conquest of Naples begins period of Austrian domination.

2000 The West celebrates the Millennium— 2,000 years since the birth of Christ.

1989 Fall of communism in Eastern Europe.

1973 World oil crisis.

1969 First man lands on the moon.

1963–1975 American war in Vietnam.

1996 Victory of Olive Tree Alliance, the first Italian government to include the former communists

1992 *Tangentopoli* scandal leads to downfall of a generation of politicians

1980 Bombing of Bologna station by right-wing terrorists.

1973–80 *Anni di Piombo*, period of terrorism in Italy.

1969–1971 *Autumno Caldo,* period of strikes and protests.

1800

1789 French Revolution begins.

1799 Napoleon becomes emperor of France.

1815 Napoleon defeated at Waterloo.

1848 Famine prompts unrest and revolutions throughout Europe.

1914–1918 World War I.

1797 Napoleon invades northern Italy.

1861 Unification of Italy.

1911 Italian invasion of Libya

1915 Italy declares war on Austria-Hungary and Germany.

1922 Fascist March on Rome.

1945 End of World War II, defeat of Germany.

1941–45 Holocaust of European Jews

1939 World War II begins.

1929 Wall Street Crash, beginning of the Great Depression.

1950

1946 Italy becomes a republic.

1943 Mussolini arrested. Italy joins side of the Allies.

1939 Italy enters the war on the side of Japan and Germany.

1936 Italy invades Ethiopia.

Glossary

Abbreviation: Ital. = Italian

Alpine: Of the Alps Mountains in northern Italy.

Baroque: Style of art and architecture originating in Italy in the 16th century and characterized by extravagant contrasts of light and shade and elaborate decoration.

Byzantine: Style of art and architecture from ancient Byzantium (now Istanbul), which emerged in the fourth century A.D. Byzantine art mixed late Roman styles with early Christian symbolism and themes.

capitalism: An economic system based on supply and demand, and private ownership of businesses and industry.

cathedral: A large and important church.

Chamber of Deputies: The lower house of the Italian parliament.

city-state: A city that is in effect an independent country with no allegiance to any larger region.

comune (**Ital.**): The standard administrative district in Italy; also the name of the local town hall.

communism: A social and political system based on a planned economy in which goods and land are owned by everyone and in which there is no private property.

democracy: A country where the people choose their government by election, and where they hold supreme power.

doge: Head of state in the historical Venetian Republic.

duomo (**Ital.**): Cathedral.

European Union (EU): An organization made up of European countries that work together on many economic, social, and political issues.

fascist: Pertaining to the fascist party of Benito Mussolini, which came to power in 1922 in Italy and adopted an authoritarian, repressive regime, based on a planned economy.

Gothic: Style of art and architecture originating in Italy in the 12th century. Largely religious in subject matter, characterized by formal depictions of the human figure and (in architecture) by soaring, intricately carved stone structures, it became the accepted style for Christian art in Western Europe for several hundred years.

lira: The Italian currency.

left-wing: Descriptive of political ideas, parties, or individuals who support a social system based on equality of wealth and opportunity and a more liberal social program, also supportive of more government control in business and social legislation.

mafia: Criminal organization operating in southern Italy with historical links to the feudal system of the region.

mafioso (**Ital.**): (plural: *mafiosi*) Member of the mafia.

mezzogiorno (**Ital.**): (Literally "midday") the south of Italy.

nationalism: Intense belief in importance of one nation's interests.

open market: A market without tariffs (a charge imposed by government to limit certain types of trade) or other trade barriers.

palazzo (**Ital**): Either a palace or an apartment house.

papacy: The office of the pope in Rome.

Papal States: The region of Italy controlled by the church between the fall of the Roman empire and the establishment of the Italian republic.

PDS (Ital.): Acronym for the *Partito Democratico della Sinistra* (Democratic Party of the Left), the former Italian Communist Party and currently the largest left-wing party in the country.

piazza: A large open square.

pietà (**Ital.**): (Literally "pity") Sculpture or painting depicting the Virgin Mary supporting the dead Christ.

Renaissance: The great revival of the arts and learning in Europe during the 14th to 16th centuries that built on a rediscovery of the arts of ancient Greece and Rome.

republic: A government in which the citizens of a country hold supreme power and where all citizens are equal under the law.

right wing: Descriptive of political ideas, parties, or individuals who support a more conservative approach to social matters and generally a less regulated approach to business.

***Risorgimento* (Ital.):** Nineteenth-century Italian movement for independence from foreign rule.

Senate: The upper house of Italy's parliament.

socialism: A social system involving the public ownership of goods and land. Less extreme than communism, it usually requires an element of democratic decision-making, rather than policy being imposed by the government or a small group of individuals.

***Tangentopoli* (Ital. "Bribesville")** Italian corruption scandal of the early 1990s initially centered at Milan.

Vatican: The center of the Catholic church in Rome and home of the pope.

Bibliography

Major Sources Used for This Book
Ginsborg, Paul, *History of Contemporary Italy*. New York: Penguin, 1990.
Procacci, Guiliano. *History of the Italian People*. New York: HarperCollins, 1987
Richards, Charles. *The New Italians*. London: Penguin, 1992.
The Economist. *Pocket World in Figures*. London: Profile Books, 2000.
Encyclopedia Britannica

General Further Reading
Encyclopedia of World Cultures. ed. Lynda A. Bennett; Boston: G.K. Hall & Co., 1992.
World Reference Atlas. London: Dorling Kindersley, 2000.
The Kingfisher History Encyclopedia. New York: Kingfisher, 1999.
Student Atlas. New York: Dorling Kindersley, 1998.
The World Book Encyclopedia. Chicago: Scott Fetzer Company, 1999.

Further Reading About Italy
Barzini, Luigi. *The Italians*. New York: Penguin, 1964.
Hibbert, Christopher. *Rome: Biography of a City*. London: Penguin, 1985
Levi, Carlo. *Christ Stopped at Eboli*. New York: Penguin, 1982.
Vasari, Giorgio. *Lives of the Artists*. New York: Penguin, 1965.

Some Websites About Italy
www.italyontheweb.org
www.italyemb.org
www.italcult.net/en/index.html
www.arca.net/uffizi/index.htm
www.italcuisine.it/
www.italyitalymagazine.com
www.made-in-italy.com
www.dolcevita.com

Index

Acknowledgments

Cover Photo Credits
Stone: (Positano, Campania); **AKG London** (Etruscan tomb painting); **Corbis:** Araldo de Luca (Michelangelo's *Pietà*)

Photo Credits
AKG London: 48, 53, 67, 71 **AKG Berlin:** S.Domingie 62, 96 British Library 63, Erich Lessing 51, 54, 94, 97, 101 **Corbis:** 102, Roger Antrobus 6, Araldo de Luca 98, Archivio Iconografico, SA 57, Jonathan Blair 24, 88 John Heseltine 37, L. Amos James 42, Robert Landau 18, Maurizio Lanini 32,

David Lees 29, 95, 103, 104, Massimo Listri 61, Frank Owen 1, 40, Vittoriano Rastelli 84, 106, 115, Galen Rowell 21, Kevin Schafer 19, David Turnley 118, **Fiat:** 86, **Hulton Getty:** 73, **Hutchison:** John Egan 23, Robert Aberman 105, J. Davey 113, Robert Francis 78, Trevor Page 109, **Peter Newark's Pictures:** 64, **Robert Hunt Library:** 70, 72, **Stone:** Doug Armand 17, Joe Cornish 12, 33, 35, Robert Everts 117, Louis Grandadam 39, Nick Gunderson 22, Simon Huber 46, 111, Manfred Mehlig 16, Simon Watson 43, Randy Wells 26, Chris Windsor 92